PRAISE FOR
THE MARKETING

'A game changer for marketers, this book is full of practical tips and frameworks for embracing the complexity of brand management and enabling true value and impact.' **Gemma Greaves, Chief Executive, The Marketing Society**

'This book gets to the heart of how brands and branding really work in a complex and ambiguous world. In a dumbed-down and soundbite culture, Lury makes a great case for why we must think harder and deeper about the purpose and philosophy behind our brands if we want them to thrive.' **Matt Close, Executive Vice President, Global Ice Cream, Unilever**

'Finally we have something that directly tackles the multiplicity and complexity of the world of brands and marketing. While there has been a long-standing recognition that marketing is not just about promotion and advertising, there has still remained a widespread appeal to reduce everything down to bite-sized slogans and one-dimensional consumers. We know that complex human behaviour is now more readily understood with the help of analytics available to us, yet many organizations still wrongly consider marketing in the narrowest sense as a functional task to be completed. The careful management of a range of relationships with stakeholders who each have differing needs, drivers and motivations is something that Giles Lury recognizes when he talks about the brand DNA being the long-term, stable brand philosophy and a key element of a multipart framework. The "how to sell a rainbow" analogy is highly valuable in making complex areas of multiplicity accessible.' **Dr Kellie Vincent, Principal Lecturer and MBA Director, Westminster Business School**

'Both accessible and persuasive in its quest to encourage marketers to move away from seeking to simplify brands and instead think about them as multifaceted entities.' **David Iddiols, Founder, HPI Research Group**

'I loved this book. As a wizened marketer who has been marketing for over 25 years, I like the refreshing challenge of core marketing convention and principles. *The Marketing Complex* confronts the traditional concept that simplicity and focus are king. It is fine, indeed good, not to be simplistic; not to be wholly single-minded. The stark reality is that brands must appeal to multiple and increasingly fragmented audiences, if not to individuals (aren't we all different, all individuals?) through several marketing propositions, whilst remaining true to their fundamental, deep-rooted principles. This is captured in a framework, "the Marketing Complex Framework" that accepts and enables both these requirements.' **Andy Beattie, Global Chief Marketing Officer, Petronas Lubricants International**

The Marketing Complex

Why modern marketers need to manage multiplicity

Giles Lury

KoganPage

First published in Great Britain and the United States in 2017 by Kogan Page Limited

2nd Floor, 45 Gee Street	c/o Martin P Hill Consulting	4737/23 Ansari Road
London EC1V 3RS	122 W 27th St, 10th Floor	Daryaganj
United Kingdom	New York, NY 10001	New Delhi 110002
www.koganpage.com	USA	India

© Giles Lury, 2017

The right of Giles Lury to be identified as the author of this work has been asserted by him in accordance with the Copyright, Designs and Patents Act 1988.

ISBN   978 0 7494 8112 4
E-ISBN 978 0 7494 8113 1

British Library Cataloguing-in-Publication Data

A CIP record for this book is available from the British Library.

Library of Congress Cataloging-in-Publication Data

Names: Lury, Giles, author.
Title: The marketing complex : why modern marketers need to manage
    multiplicity / Giles Lury.
Description: London ; New York : Kogan Page, [2017] | Includes
    bibliographical references and index.
Identifiers: LCCN 2017028570 (print) | LCCN 2017035158 (ebook) | ISBN
    9780749481131 (ebook) | ISBN 9780749481124 (alk. paper)
Subjects: LCSH: Marketing. | Branding (Marketing)
Classification: LCC HF5415 (ebook) | LCC HF5415 .L8168 2017 (print) | DDC
    658.8–dc23

Typeset by Integra Software Services, Pondicherry
Print production managed by Jellyfish
Printed and bound by CPI Group (UK) Ltd, Croydon, CR0 4YY

For my late Mum and Dad.
Much loved and sorely missed.

CONTENTS

PREFACE

In 1979, over 20 years after they were married, my dad gave my mum a Valentine's card. It was an old 1920s style illustrated postcard of a boy giving his girl a big envelope with 'To my Valentine' on it.

Along with it, my dad gave my mum a piece of paper with the following typed on it:

Correspondence between aspiring poet and creative writer

Be mine, Be mine,

Please be my Valentine.

An ardent lover would not bother with please.

Be mine, Be mine

Be my Valentine.

As your poem will arrive on 14th February, you reflect adversely on your recipient's intelligence by referring explicitly to Valentine.

Be mine, Be mine

Poetry should concentrate and distil. Why this repetition?

Be mine.

This possessive attitude is outmoded; an unpleasant residue of male chauvinism.

Be.

Ah, I like this. Concise, but full of implications. Yes, I think this will do.

Message sent:

Be mine, be mine,

Please be my Valentine.

Little did I realize that this would not only be an enduring memory of the love my parents shared but a wonderful example of the siren call of oversimplification, something about which I would write a book, this book.

ACKNOWLEDGEMENTS

'*I see you.*'
FROM THE FILM *AVATAR*, 2009,
DIRECTED, WRITTEN, PRODUCED AND CO-EDITED
BY JAMES CAMERON

With regard to this book, as with any book, there are many people I must thank for their time, comments and, yes, criticisms. Constructive criticism is not always something I like but it is something that I do actually appreciate. Without all the people I am going to mention, this book would never have come to pass; with them, it is undoubtedly better than it would otherwise have been.

Firstly, my thanks go to everyone at The Value Engineers, colleagues past and present, who gave me their time and thoughts, their challenges and builds. Though it seems slightly unfair, I would like to call out two in particular. Paul Gaskell, who 'got' what I was talking about immediately, encouraged me to develop my thinking and helped give me the time to write this book. I have seen him present the framework and the thinking behind it numerous times and wonder whether he should, perhaps, have written the book instead of me. The other person is Alan Morrison, who now works for Sverige Radio, but was probably the very first person who had to work with me in persuading a client that using this model would help them. I'm pleased to say it did.

I want to thank the growing number of clients who have bought into and have used the model successfully. I'm grateful to the brands and writers who have given permission for us to reprint quotes and/ or use their logos. It is much appreciated. I always prefer a textbook to have pictures and figures.

I also want to thank the team at Kogan Page, Jenny, Charlotte, Philippa and Ro'isin for their belief, hard work and encouragement. I hope for all your sakes as well as mine that the book is the success we hope it will be.

I want to thank my wife Karen and my family who put up with me writing the book and the various mood swings that went with that. In particular, I want to thank Callum, one of my sons, who though not a marketer not only read the earliest drafts but gave me frank and fresh comments, many of which I have incorporated into later drafts of the text.

So to everyone, including you dear reader, as the Na'vi might say, 'I see you.'

Introduction

It almost goes without saying that the marketing world has changed fundamentally since the heady days of the *Madmen*.

Almost; because despite the fact that we now live in a digital era where brands need to cross categories, continents and customers and engage with them all 24/7, too much brand thinking is still based on old-world principles.

It was 70 years ago, at the beginning of the *Madmen* era, that Rosser Reeves suggested that humans were only able to take out one key message from a piece of advertising and the Unique Selling Proposition (the USP) was born.

In 1981, Al Ries and Jack Trout in their now famous book *Positioning – the battle for your mind*, said: 'In an over-communicated world, you need an oversimplified message.' It suited advertising agencies, their favoured medium the 30-second commercial and what is now known as 'interruption marketing', so their idea spread becoming the mantra behind much of marketing theory and many of the tools developed, and still used by marketers today.

Its use has been further entrenched by more recent trends like the 'cash rich, time poor' phenomenon, the continued growth of a 'sound-bite society' and the widely used notion of KISS – Keep it simple, stupid.

At the same time, brand owners are abdicating their responsibilities and handing over the reins to consumers and customers. 'The customer is king' is another pillar of modern branding and brand owners appear to be rushing to hand them their crown jewels, their brands. Witness the emergence of Chief Customer Officers, the explosion in 'co-creation' and the growth of customer closeness programmes.

While I will suggest that this may be sensible, even desirable for marketing, I will argue that this is not the case for branding and brand positioning. The difference between branding and marketing has been lost and too few realize that brands need what George H W Bush famously called 'the vision thing'. While many may appear to recognize the potential of a brand purpose, setting these by asking your customers is often limiting and even dangerous. Furthermore, the notion that these can be underpinned by all-too-often generic values rather than by real principles is the cause of blandness not brand-ness.

It is time for the marketing world and brand owners to realize that in the new brandscape being single-minded can equate to being narrow-minded. For too long marketers have been seduced by what I call the siren call of simplicity. In this new era, they must recognize the difference between simplifying and simplistic. They need to realize the risk of oversimplification and the danger of driving to singularities. It is time for them to recognize the difference between marketing and branding and that while being customer centric is key to great marketing, the best brands come from within.

This book sets out for both: the need for marketers to take back ownership of their brands and to embrace the need to manage the multiplicity of these valuable assets.

The Marketing Complex will aim to be provocative. Its objective is to spark debate, to challenge conventional wisdom, and to encourage marketers to recognize the power of depth and variety rather than focusing on the narrow-mindedness that singularity can bring.

It aims to clearly differentiate marketing from branding and to demonstrate why this is so important in shaping our future approach to both.

It provides a new multidimensional framework – the Marketing Complex Framework, some tools and techniques, a number of examples and shows how these can help marketers build richer, fuller brands.

The first four chapters will outline the case for a change in marketers' mindset.

Chapter 1 will explore the origins and appeal of simplification from the USP, through Ries and Trout's argument for oversimplification to the continuing obsession with single-minded thinking. I will identify the reasons for its appeal but highlight some of the weaknesses and lack of scientific evidence to support these hypotheses.

Chapter 2 will briefly set out some of the fundamental changes in the world of branding, media and customer expectations, and how these have led to the need to develop a more flexible and multidimensional approach to positioning.

Chapter 3 will address the current preoccupation with the notion of consumers as 'owners' of the brand and the dangers this brings. It will highlight the difference between branding and marketing and why customers may be royalty in marketing but the best brands can be seen as closer to religions, coming from within and based on beliefs and principles.

Chapter 4 will explore and define marketing and branding, independently and in relation to each other, demonstrating the difference between the two. It will support the need for marketing to be customer led but suggest that brands need 'that vision thing'. It will suggest brands need to be customer fed not customer led and certainly not customer owned.

Chapter 5 will pull all the arguments from the previous chapters together and make the case for multiplicity – how brand positioning itself needs to be repositioned.

Chapter 6 will introduce a two-part brand framework based on a brand philosophy and a series of go-to-market propositions. Its aim is to provide a practical means for marketers to codify and manage multiplicity. It will introduce the framework and provide an example on how it works in practice.

Chapters 7 and 8 will look at the two sections of the framework in more detail. Firstly, Chapter 7 looks at the brand philosophy. It will make the case for a more holistic and richer expression of any brand vision or purpose. It will suggest that this may benefit from being a higher-order purpose as suggested in much of the current marketing literature but also a deeper, wider concept which allows for a broader narrative. It will explain why values aren't as valuable as principles and beliefs. It will use analysis by the author and The Value Engineers based on Interbrand's 100 most valuable brands to show that the same values come up time and time again and the ones chosen tend to be bland and generic, 'motherhood and apple pie' statements. I will argue that it has been too easy for brands to 'sign' up to loose values, which are easy to agree to but which are difficult to measure and don't provide real parameters for brand behaviour. I will aim to demonstrate how the use of beliefs and principles can be more brand-specific and provide something for those brands to live up to and be measured by.

Chapter 8 will explore the second section of the framework, the go-to-market propositions. It will review different types of propositions and the elements that make them up. It draws the important distinction between features and benefits and goes on to provide practical tools for helping construct propositions, including benefit laddering.

Next, in Chapter 9, I will explore the implications for marketers' mindset. I will suggest that branding remains a combination of an art and science but that marketers need to embrace ambiguity and learn how to manage different perspectives simultaneously.

Chapter 10 will provide an overview and conclusions. It will identify areas and challenges that the book raises but doesn't necessarily explore. It will finish with a challenge for marketers and brand owners to think differently, to embrace multiplicity and to 'keep it complex, stupid'.

The final, short chapter asks the question, 'What's next?'. It challenges the reader to engage in the debate and take the thinking in this book onwards and hopefully upwards.

The siren call of simplicity

'That's simply beautiful,' said the customer.
'Yes and beautifully simple too,' said the salesman.
'But devilishly difficult under the skin,' said the brand owner, quietly.

The soundbite society

We live in a 'soundbite' society.

While the term's origins can be traced back to the 1980s, when it was first applied to a number of Ronald Reagan's short and often memorable phrases, there are many examples of soundbites that clearly predate that period. Peggy Noonan, the author, columnist, speechwriter and sometime special advisor to Ronald Reagan, describes a soundbite as speakers 'simply trying in words to capture the essence of the thought they wished to communicate.'

She suggests that the most famous phrase in Franklin D Roosevelt's first Inaugural Address in March 1933, 'The only thing we have to fear is fear itself' was a much earlier example of a political soundbite. These short, sharp, highly memorable phrases that simplify often more complex thoughts are now in everyday use.

Examples can be seen in newspaper headlines, of which *The Sun*, the UK's leading tabloid, is perhaps the best exponent. Around the time of the EU referendum, it carried the following headlines:

'Queen backs Brexit' 9 March 2017

'Be-LEAVE in Britain' 14 June 2017

'See EU later' 24 June 2017

Advertising taglines would seem to be a variation on the theme, too: short, engaging and designed to capture attention.

Following this explosion in the use of soundbites, opinion is divided on their impact on the quality and clarity of communication. For some it perfectly reflects the need to quickly engage and attract an audience. For others, like Jeffrey Scheuer, it is part of the dumbing down of politics and indeed society. In his book, *The Soundbite Society*, Scheuer argues that the soundbite was the product of television's increased power over all other forms of communication, and that the resulting trend towards short, catchy snippets of information has had a significant negative impact on US political discourse, the argument being that due to its brevity, the soundbite often ignores or oversimplifies the broader context so can often be misleading or inaccurate.

It would, however, appear that the proponents of its use are in the ascendency and that underlying this is the widespread appeal of simplicity. Look on the internet and there are thousands of quotes, expressions and indeed many soundbites championing the beauty of simplicity. Its proponents stretch as far back as Cicero who conceived it as an ingredient of elegance.

Famous authors, artists and business 'stars' are fans of simplification:

'That's been one of my mantras – focus and simplicity. Simple can be harder than complex: You have to work hard to get your thinking clean to make it simple. But it's worth it in the end because once you get there, you can move mountains.'

Steve Jobs

'Complexity is your enemy. Any fool can make something complicated. It is hard to make something simple.'

Richard Branson

'The greatest ideas are the simplest.'

William Golding

The increasing appeal of this need for simplicity and brevity may also be the result of another term coined in the late 20th century, that of being 'cash-rich, time poor'. Whether or not this engaging soundbite is actually true of today's society is irrelevant, as in this case perception is reality in the eye of the beholder. Numerous studies have shown that people today feel that they never have enough time, even if modern technology and convenience products mean that, in fact, they have much more spare time than previous generations did. This generation wants it all, they want it now and many aren't prepared to wait or work too hard for it, so keep it short, keep it simple – or to simplify 'Keep it simple, stupid'.

KISS, the acronym of 'Keep it simple, stupid', was a design principle used by the US Navy in the 1960s and associated with aircraft engineer, Kelly Johnson. The KISS principle states that most systems work best if they are kept simple rather than made more complicated. Therefore, simplicity should be a key goal in any design and unnecessary complexity should be avoided.

A political variation is attributed to James Carville, campaign strategist for Bill Clinton during the 1992 US presidential campaign. He created the phrase 'It's the economy, stupid'. It was directed at Clinton's campaign workers as a key message to focus on but became much more widely known and used. (Interestingly, it was not the only core message. There were in fact three core messages, the other two being 'Change vs. more of the same' and 'Don't forget healthcare'.)

The growth of singularity

Perhaps, not surprisingly given this history, design, journalism and politics are three disciplines that continue to champion simplicity and soundbites. Another is marketing, where the mantra is perhaps not just about the beauty of simplicity, but also its power to help persuade. Marketing has, however, taken it a stage further and, in many instances, focused on singularities. It aims to simplify things down to a single thought, a single target group or in some instances a single word.

Marketing and advertising's particular attraction to this extreme version of simplicity can be traced back to three men, the three founding fathers of singularity.

The first 'father' took a somewhat colourful route into his marketing career, originally as a copywriter and ultimately as Chair of one of the world's largest ad agencies. The son of a Methodist preacher, Rosser Reeves was born in 1910 in Danville, Virginia. He went to University of Virginia but was there only briefly before being expelled for drunkenly crashing a friend's car, an event made even worse by the fact that this was 1929 and the Prohibition era.

Luckily, for him, he had just won the US $100 prize in a statewide chemistry contest that also served as his final exam for first year 'Chem 101'. Most other students had written serious and most probably dull essays on chemical formulae. Reeves, who having spent much of his time drinking and dancing and knowing little or nothing about the subject, wrote a rather lighter essay, which nonetheless had the appealing, engaging and clearly prize-winning title of 'Better living through chemistry'. (Not someone to waste a good idea, Reeves would later use the title as a strapline in a DuPont Corporation campaign.)

He used his prize money to move to Richmond where he got a job at a bank that had a policy of hiring winners of state competitions. They soon discovered that Reeves was a poor banker but seemed to have a way with words. They moved him to the advertising departments where he found his calling.

He moved to Cecil, Warwick & Cecil in New York, in 1934, and then like many subsequent advertising executives he moved regularly, firstly to Ruthrauff & Ryan, then Blackett-Sample-Hummert before joining Benton & Bowles. In 1940, he left to join Ted Bates where he stayed, rising through the ranks and ultimately becoming Chairman.

Already known as a successful copywriter, it was here that he would fully develop his ground-breaking notion of the Unique Selling Proposition, or as it is more commonly known the USP. The USP was, and still is a fundamental construct on which the belief in the power of simplicity in advertising is built. In fact, as the name suggests, it actually goes beyond simplicity, and with its focus on a single proposition, it introduced the notion of singularity in marketing.

The leading industry magazine *Adage* describes the development of a USP and the rules for its use in its online 'Encyclopaedia':

'To Mr Reeves, consumers were not irrational creatures driven by hidden motives even they did not understand. Instead, he said, consumers received too many messages. The challenge to advertisers was to create memorable messages that the consumer could easily understand.[1]

The USP, he said, must follow three rules:

First, the advertiser must present a definite proposition: If you buy X, you will get a specific benefit.

Second, the benefit must be unique to the particular product, unavailable in the products offered by competitors.

Third, the proposition must be a 'selling' one—that is, the benefit must be one that many people will want. (For example, Colgate toothpaste "cleans your breath while it cleans your teeth.").'

In short, a Unique Selling Proposition can be defined as the (*one*) reason a product should be bought as opposed to any of its competitors' products.

Paul Feldwick in his book *The Anatomy of Humbug*, notes:

'Reeves asserted that "the consumer tends to remember just one thing from an advertisement – one strong claim, or one strong concept".'[2]

He goes on to point out that:

'He [Reeves] produced no real evidence for this claim – and I know of none myself to support it – but it has been so often repeated ever since that it now seems to be universally believed, not least in creative departments.'[3]

In other words, the foundation for what has become one of the most widely used and most important ideas in marketing was based on one person's assertion and no real scientific evidence. It suited advertising agencies and was seductively simple, and it stuck.

It is, however, really quite extraordinary how much credence is given to the assertion considering the absence of any real validation and the fact that there is much evidence to demonstrate that it simply isn't true. Despite this, Reeves' position as one of the fathers of modern advertising remains, and his other claims to fame include the fact that he was a published poet, wrote a well-respected book on shooting pool and, more recently, that he is one model for the professional accomplishments of the TV series *Madmen*'s lead protagonist, Don Draper.

The other two founding fathers of marketing's preoccupation with singularity both worked in the advertising department of General Electric before coming together to form an agency of their own.

Al Ries had graduated from DePauw University in 1950 with a degree in liberal arts and accepted a position with the advertising department of General Electric, before founding his own advertising agency in New York City, Ries Cappiello Colwell, in 1963.

Jack Trout, having started his career in the advertising department of General Electric, went on to become a divisional advertising manager at Uniroyal before joining Ries at Ries Cappiello Colwell, which would later change its focus to marketing strategy. It was renamed Trout & Ries. The pair would work together for more than 26 years, though now both run separate marketing strategy firms.

In 1972, they co-authored a three-part series of articles declaring the arrival of the 'Positioning Era' in *Advertising Age* magazine, promoting their new concept of positioning.

Their real impact, however, happened when they returned to these articles in 1981 and turned them into what has become a classic marketing textbook, *Positioning: The battle for your mind*. Though different from Reeves' approach in many ways, there is one striking similarity, summed up in what is probably the most quoted phrase from the book:

'In an over-communicated world, you need an oversimplified message.'[4]

Ries and Trout argued that even back in 1981, before the birth of the internet, there was so much communication that to cut through this noise and start to own a space in your customers' mind, which they said was the ultimate aim of positioning, you needed a communication that was reduced to a single-minded message.

'To succeed in our over-communicated society, a company must create a position in the mind, a position that takes into consideration not only a company's own strengths and weaknesses, but those of its competitors as well.'[5]

Ries and Trout recognized that the role of advertising wasn't exclusively as a sales tool in so far as it also built up a brand's equity – 'a position in the mind'. Their notion of positioning was to provide a more rounded and fuller view of a brand, rather than just the sales focus of Reeves' USP. However, they strongly advocated a simple and single-minded message with which to build that 'positioning'.

What the book did, therefore, was to take the drive for single-mindedness beyond advertising into the broader remit of brand strategy. It defined a 'brand positioning' as a summation of the brand's position within its market, what it offered its consumers and how the brand is differentiated from the competition and was seen as an expression of the very essence of the brand.

The classic brand model

Frameworks and models were soon being developed to capture and communicate these new brand positionings and they quickly became one of the most important documents in the marketing departments – and, in fact, still are (Figure 1.1).

These models, a series of cells, come in a whole range of shapes and sizes including onions, keys, pyramids, stamps and bridges. I worked with a brewer who had brand openers and a bakery company that had brand biscuits. While the shapes and the names of specific headings for the cells often change from company to company, from brand to brand and from agency to agency, in reality most of the brand positioning models have the same cells. In fact, many of the

Figure 1.1 A selection of different brand model shapes

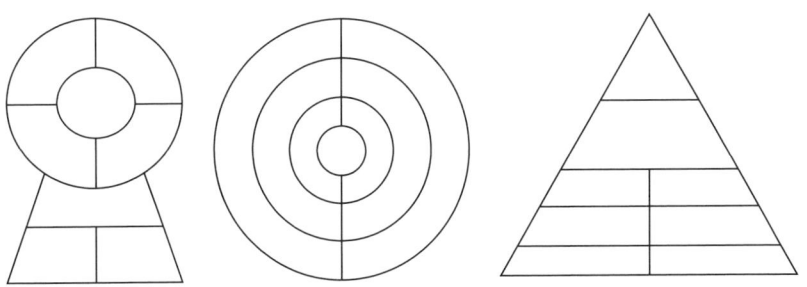

cells haven't changed with perhaps the exception of the additions of a consumer insight box and sometimes a brand purpose or vision cell. The classic cells are:

- Target audience – a description of the 'prospect', the core group of customer that brand wishes to attract. Definitions can be narrow or broad, from simple demographic descriptions to more complex behavioural and psychographic descriptions.

- Consumer insight (a later addition to original models, which was included as the notion of insight grew in the 1990s) – a penetrating understanding that gets to the real needs and motivations of the target audience so helping you to better define a motivating proposition.

- Brand proposition or promise – sometimes known as the brand promise box or the 'Godfather box', ('the offer you just can't refuse'). This should be a single-minded summation of the benefit that the brand (or more often specific product or service) delivers. In many instances a USP.

- Reasons to believe – the proof points that help substantiate any claim made in the proposition box. The facts, the assertions and the actions of the brand that help to substantiate the promise a brand makes.

- Values – normally a series of adjectives describing the ideals and the tenets to which the brand adheres. Ideally, they should be an expression of the core philosophy of the brand.

- Personality – the personification of the brand. A description of the brand as if it was human or had human characteristics; how it would behave, its attitudes and how it would interact with others. The aim of the box is to define the brand's character, style and tone of voice.

- Essence – a summation of the brand's DNA, its raison d'être. It is traditionally kept very short and is normally just two or three words, though it can sometimes be either a short sentence or alternatively just a single word.

- Differentiator – a short description of what makes the brand's proposition different from its competitors.

Given the ongoing belief in the desirability of single-mindedness, both the Essence and the Differentiator were the focus for simplification. This drive for a single-minded Essence is something that may have been reinforced by the fact that these models were often developed by advertising agencies working with marketing departments, and it was in agencies where the notion of single-mindedness had first and most strongly taken root).

Interestingly, in many agencies you will still find the belief that the best brand essences are summed up in a single thought or even a single word; for example, Volvo = safety.

The line extension trap

Brand positioning wasn't the only area of brand strategy to be influenced by Ries and Trout's book. Their thinking also stretched beyond positioning into the theory and practice of line and brand extensions.

Line (or brand) extensions are the use of an existing brand name on a new product or service entering a market or market sector that is different from the original market of that brand. For example, LEGO produce toy construction bricks but also produce children's clothing, board games, watches and use their name on theme parks.

In a chapter entitled 'The Line Extension Trap' Ries and Trout argued that stretching your brand in this way was dangerous as it diluted the single-minded positioning your brand owned in people's minds. They said that while:

> 'Logic is on the side of line extension. Arguments of economics. Trade acceptance. Consumer acceptance. Lower advertising costs. Increased income. The corporate image.
>
> Logic is on the side of line extension. Truth unfortunately is not.'[6]

They went on to quote numerous examples of line extensions that didn't work including Dial soap, Protein 21 shampoo, Lifesavers, Pall Mall cigarettes. They argued that line extension was potentially dangerous for the long-term health of a brand.

> 'A name is a rubber band. It will stretch, but not beyond a certain point. Furthermore, the more you stretch a name, the weaker it becomes. (Just the opposite of what you might expect.)'[7]

More specifically, they link a (single) product's positioning to the brand name and state that this is particularly strong when the brand name is a generic one – when the brand name becomes synonymous or a surrogate for the category; for example, Sellotape for see-through sticky tape in the United Kingdom, or Bayer for aspirin and Dial for soap in the United States.

> 'Line extension works against the generic brand position. It blurs the sharp focus of the brand in the mind. No longer can the prospect say 'Bayer' if he or she wants an aspirin. Or 'Dial' for soap.'[8]

In short they argued that a successful brand should own a very single-minded 'position in the brain', which is tied closely to one product or at most one category and that by stretching it you weaken that position.*

It is another important stage in the development and embedding of the notion that to be successful you need a single-minded brand. The implicit link between the (single) product and the brand and the danger of stretching beyond this, is as we will see something that narrows the potential for brand development.

(*To be completely fair, Ries and Trout do conclude their chapter on line extension by saying 'We call line extension a trap, not a mistake. Line extension can work if... But it's a big if. If your competitors are foolish. If your volume is small. If you have no competitors. If you don't expect to build a position in your mind. If you don't do any advertising.' Hardly the most ringing endorsement but not a complete No-No.)

Singularization

This acceptance of the desirability of single-mindedness and the power of simplicity continued and spread, leading to further 'singularization' of marketing.

People may no longer talk about the USP, yet many creative briefs still contain a 'what is the single most important thing we want people to take form this advertisement' section. Creatives and their clients like to talk about *the* big idea (though admittedly the latter may be executed in and across a variety of media and campaigns).

There is still *the* core target audience and some companies like to personify this as *single* individual. Many companies are looking for *the* killer insight to drive their innovations. They like to focus their ideation around **an** insight that they hope will deliver the Aha-kerching! – the revelation translated into a money spinning concept – for the next big thing. Some companies will only innovate if and when they have a verified insight, believing the only way to do innovation is to be consumer led. Despite the explosion in 'big data', or maybe because of it there seems to be a simultaneous trend in marketing analytics towards a focus on *single* figure scores especially NPS (Net Promoter Score).

The same sort of thinking manifests itself again in the field of innovation with the preoccupation with the 'eureka' moment – the one blinding flash of inspiration when the metaphorical lightbulb goes on.

This simplification may make a marketer's job easier but for today's complex world that is just too many definite articles and simply too much simplification. It is not just simplification, it is oversimplification.

But not any simpler

Returning to those quotes about simplicity mentioned earlier in the chapter, buried among all the others there is one attributed to Albert Einstein which, like many of his quotes, contains a great deal of sense. He, too, was a fan of simplicity, but he knew that there are limits to simplification. What he said was: 'Everything should be made as simple as possible… but not any simpler'. It is a more complex idea than just a direct call to simplify everything but it is actually all the better for it. What he was challenging was the siren call of oversimplification.

Reeves' premise of 'the consumer tends to remember just one thing from an advertisement – one strong claim, or one strong concept' is not only unsupported by any scientific evidence, it contradicts my experience of every advertising tracking study I have ever seen (and in my 30 years' career that's quite a few).

More scientifically, it also goes against what is often called Miller's law.[9] Miller's law comes from one of the most highly cited papers in Psychology, 'The Magical Number Seven, Plus or Minus Two: Some limits on our capacity for processing information'. The cognitive psychologist, George A Miller of Princeton University's Department of Psychology, in *Psychological Review*, published it in 1956. It states that the number of objects an average human can hold in working memory is 7 ± 2.

More recently there have been papers published, including one by Nelson Cowan, Jeff Rouder and Richard More in the journal *Proceedings of the National Academy of Sciences* on 14 April 2008, that have suggested a lower limit of only three or four.[10]

The potential and indeed the 'power' of three is a well-known concept in storytelling and is an approach that is very popular with brands. The power of three manifests itself in stories with three central characters, including the likes of *The Three Musketeers*, *The Three Stooges*, *The Three Amigos*, *Three Men and a Baby*, *The Three Little Pigs* as well as *Goldilocks and the Three Bears*. Equally, it is used to emphasize and make a point: 'You've let the school down; you've let me down; and you've let yourself down.' (And, as will be shown later, there are a number of famous brand visions or purposes that are three-pronged.)

Whether it is three, four, five, seven or nine, all of these are more than the original one presented by Rosser Reeves. At the other extreme, the BBC reported that a 24-year-old Chinese graduate student memorized 67,980 digits of Pi which he recited in 2005 during a 24-hour stretch without so much as a bathroom break, breaking the world record.

'The fallacy of the single cause' is another relevant scientific term. It is also known as causal oversimplification, causal reductionism and reduction fallacy, and manifests itself when it is assumed that there is a single, simple cause of an outcome, when in reality a number of different and sometimes interdependent causes may have led to that outcome.

It results in the sort of thinking that because X occurred after Y then Y must have caused X. Simple but not necessarily correct. One example might be when a scientist electrically stimulates one area of the brain, observes an effect (say, the patient blinks his or her eyes), and assumes that the brain area is sufficient for the movement (the essence of blinking) rather than merely necessary.

It translates in modern culture and into the media with the posing of questions such as: 'What was the cause of this?'; 'What is the one thing we should do to stop this happening again?'; the inference being that there is one cause, one change or one factor responsible when in reality there are probably a large number of contributing factors.

As for the one blinding flash of inspiration, in his recent work *Where Good Ideas Come From*, the author Steven Johnson identifies the importance of what he calls the 'slow hunch' and the truth that the best ideas often have multiple sources:

> 'Breakthrough ideas almost never come in a moment of great insight. Most important ideas take a long time to evolve. They spend a long time dormant at the background. It isn't until the idea has had 2 or 3 years, sometimes 10 or 20 years to mature that it suddenly becomes accessible to you and useful to you... and this is because good ideas usually come from the collision of smaller hunches so that they form something bigger than themselves.'[11]

Managing multiplicity

What then is the alternative to oversimplification?

In a complex world, there is a danger that being single-minded is in fact being narrow-minded and I believe that, in fact, rather than simplicity, the marketing world needs to embrace and manage multiplicity. Multiplicity is a concept that you can find in mathematics, philosophy, chemistry, software, media studies and psychology.

For example, in psychology multiplicity is the term used to describe the everyday use of multiple personalities by a single person. What this means is that a person may adopt a kind, nurturing personality when dealing with their children but change to a more aggressive, forceful personality when working as a high-flying executive.

I am one person and yet play many roles with different 'target audiences'; at work I'm both a challenging and a collaborative colleague, with clients I'm hopefully a stimulating solution provider, with my family I'm a firm but fair father (my description not my children's), with my wife I'm a companion and husband, with old friends... I'm not sure I would want to be summed up in one PowerPoint slide, let alone one word!

The idea of psychological multiplicity is also expressed in the following short meme about being a dad:

> He can play like a kid
>
> Give advice like a friend
>
> And protect like a bodyguard

What is particularly interesting about this concept is that it resonates with two key marketing tenants. Firstly, the notion of need-states and, secondly, the often used comparison between brand and a person.

Need-states, one of the few areas of marketing which does seem to have embraced multiplicity, are a concept developed by Wendy Gordon. They are described in her 1994 book *Goodthinking* where she notes that there are often more differences between the same person making a brand choice on two separate occasions than there are between two different people making the same brand choice on the same occasion.[12]

Alternatively, they can be defined as 'The me that I am when...', a direct interpretation of the psychological multiplicity, recognizing that the one entity – in this case a person – manifests themselves in many different ways without being schizophrenic.

One of the reasons that this is so interesting is that marketers seem to be able to accept this for people but not for brands, yet this similarity between a brand and a person is one that is often made. Stephen King, the ex-JWT Chairman, drew the analogy in his famous paper 'What is a brand?'.[13]

People are complex and multifaceted, which is why they are so interesting and engaging, and I would contend the same is true of brands. A unidimensional monotone brand is likely to be a very dull and unengaging brand.

Other analogies that could be made would be between a brand and a novel or a brand and a piece of music; so whether it is plots, characters, twists and turns or whether it is melodies, baselines, vocals and harmonies, the writers and authors are managers and conduct their constructs of multiplicity.

Brands should be unique and complex, and the current tendency to oversimplification may help them to be easier to grasp but it can be a false god for their marketers. Brands need to embrace, and in fact benefit from embracing, complexity, not ignoring it or oversimplifying it. A modern brand owner therefore needs to be a brand 'conductor' or 'editor'.

In conclusion

This first chapter has set out the almost magnetic appeal of simplicity and how this has led to a soundbite society, where there is often a desire to KISS (Keep it simple, stupid).

I have looked at how simplicity has also been entrenched in marketing, and traced the emergence of what I have called 'singularity', an unfounded fixation on oversimplification and a desire to reduce everything to a single focus.

The stories of the three 'fathers' of singularity, Reeves, Ries and Trout have been told. They cover how the thinking they developed was initially focused on advertising but spread into brand strategy, driven in particular by Ries and Trout's concern with the 'line extension trap' and the dangers of blurring of a brand's sharp focus.

While agreeing that simplification is desirable, I have argued that it often leads to oversimplification and so suggest marketing needs to consider a notion summed up in a quote from Einstein: 'Everything should be made as simple as possible … but not any simpler'.

I have discussed some of the scientific arguments that counter the notion of singularity, including Miller's law and the fallacy of the single cause.

The idea of managing multiplicity has been introduced. I have noted that it exists in many other disciplines and have drawn a link between psychological multiplicity and need-states, one of the few areas where marketing seems to have adopted some elements of multiplicity.

Finally, I have used the parallel between a brand and a person to demonstrate the inappropriateness of trying to sum up a brand in a word or a PowerPoint slide.

Notes

1 Reeves, R (2003) [accessed 10 January 2017] Reeves, Rosser (1910–1984), *Adage*, [Online] http://adage.com/article/adage-encyclopedia/reeves-rosser-1910-1984/98848/

2 Feldwick, P (2015) *The Anatomy of Humbug: How to think differently about advertising*, Matador, Leicester

3 Feldwick, P (2015) *The Anatomy of Humbug: How to think differently about advertising*, Matador, Leicester

4 Ries, A and Trout, J (2001) *Positioning: The battle for your mind*, McGraw-Hill Education, London

5 Ries, A and Trout, J (2001) *Positioning: The battle for your mind*, McGraw-Hill Education, London

6 Ries, A and Trout, J (2001) *Positioning: The battle for your mind*, McGraw-Hill Education, London

7 Ries, A and Trout, J (2001) *Positioning: The battle for your mind*, McGraw-Hill Education, London

8 Ries, A and Trout, J (2001) *Positioning: The battle for your mind*, McGraw-Hill Education, London

9 Miller, A G (1956) The Magical Number Seven, Plus or Minus Two: Some limits on our capacity for processing information, *Psychological Review* [Online] http://www.psych.utoronto.ca/users/peterson/psy430s2001/Miller%20GA%20Magical%20Seven%20Psych%20Review%201955.pdf

10 Cowan, N, Morey, C C, Morey D R, Pratte, S M, Rouder, N J and Zwilling, E C (2008) [accessed 10 January 2017] An assessment of fixed-capacity models of visual working memory, *Proceedings of the National Academy of Sciences of the United States of America* [Online] http://www.pnas.org/content/105/16/5975.full

11 Johnson, S (2011) *Where Good Ideas Come From: The seven patterns of innovation*, Penguin, London

12 Gordon, W (1994) *Goodthinking: A guide to qualitative research*, NTC Publications, Australia

13 King, S (1971) [accessed 10 January 2017] Stephen King 1971: What is a brand? The definitive essay on brand building, with a foreword by Guy Murphy, *Campaign* [Online] http://www.campaignlive.co.uk/article/743160/stephen-king-1971-brand

A new brandscape

'He had been thinking of how landscape moulds a language.

It was impossible to imagine these hills giving forth anything but the soft syllables of Irish, just as only certain forms of German could be spoken on the high crags of Europe; or Dutch in the muddy, guttural, phlegmish lowlands.'

ALEXANDER MCCALL SMITH

The spread of branding

While some examples of branding can be traced right back to the Roman Empire, the practice first came to the fore as a mark of ownership, with cattlemen branding their herds with their own distinctive marks to denote their ownership in the 19th century.

However, branding has really come a long way in the last 200 years. The birth of modern branding coincides with the British Industrial Revolution, which helped create both mass production and mass consumption. In this new era, branding evolved to become a mark of who the manufacturer was, and a guarantee of the consistent quality of their product.

In a speech to the Advertising Association of Great Britain in 1996, the then Chairman of Unilever, Sir Michael Perry, told the story of Sunlight soap, explaining the rationale behind this move.

'When William Hesketh Lever first packaged up his Sunlight soap, he had a clear sense of what he was offering to Lancashire housewives. It was a reassuring guarantee of predictability and consistency.

It wasn't possible for the housewife to get the equivalent guarantee elsewhere.

Certainly not when she purchased a lump of soap, which had been of a block of unknown origin and uncertain quality in a grocer's store. William Hesketh Lever's simple brand guarantee was a foundation of a world-wide integrated business – from the palm tree to the soap kettle as he put it'.[1]

Not only is this an example of one of the first uses of branding in its modern commercial sense, but it has led to one of the most widely used definitions of a brand.

Philip Kotler in his classic marketing textbook *Managing Markets* defines a brand as:

'A name, term, symbol or design, or a combination of them, which is intended to signify the goods or services of one seller or group of sellers and to differentiate them from those of competitors.'[2]

Nowadays the *Collins Concise English Dictionary* includes numerous definitions for 'brand', a number of which reflect Kotler's definition. They include:

'An identifying mark made, usually by burning on the skin of animals or formerly slaves or criminals, especially as a proof of ownership.

A particular product or a characteristic that serves to identify a particular product.

A trade name or trademark.'[3]

As more and more products were 'branded' and competition grew, there was a rapidly growing need for manufacturers to differentiate the brands they made against all the other newly emerging brands, not just from unbranded commodities – the 'block[s] of unknown origin and uncertain quality in a grocer's store'. They needed not only to be seen and known by their names but they needed to differentiate the promises they made.

Marketing moved into the era of the Unique Selling Proposition. From there, driven by the thinking of Ries and Trout, it moved in the world of 'positioning'.

A model that this suggests for the creation of a brand is a traditional 'product plus' model (see Figure 2.1). First, you start with a product to which you add a name, an identity, a set of 'values' (the

Figure 2.1 The classic 'Product Plus' model of brand development

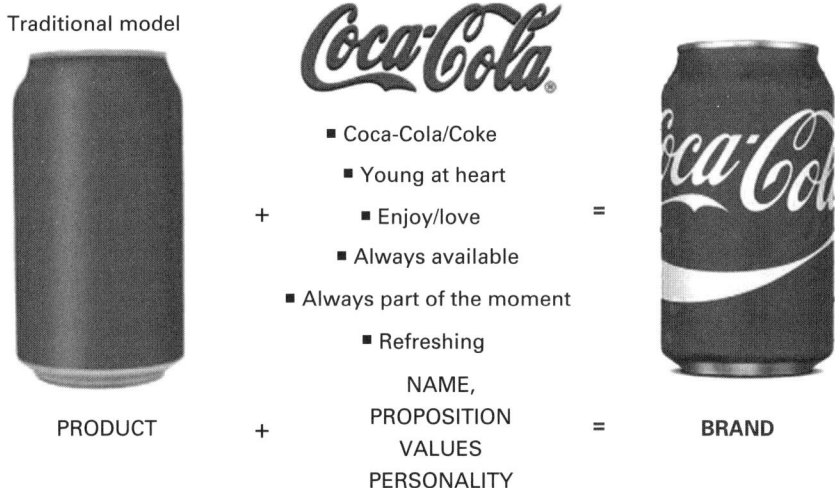

Traditional model

PRODUCT + NAME, PROPOSITION VALUES PERSONALITY = BRAND

- Coca-Cola/Coke
- Young at heart
- Enjoy/love
- Always available
- Always part of the moment
- Refreshing

SOURCE The Value Engineers. With thanks to Coca-Cola UK

ideals and the tenets to which the brand adheres) and a proposition that you communicate via advertising thereby creating your brand.

However, two assumptions implicitly underpin the thinking behind the model:

- The first is that the heartland of the thinking about branding is rooted in fast-moving consumer goods (FMCG). As mentioned above, the model starts with a product, a commodity and through the addition of name, proposition, values and personality transforms itself into a brand.

- The second is that the proposition is directly linked to the product. The inference is that brands are single product brands and eschew Ries and Trout's 'trap' of line extensions. They don't weaken their brand or 'confuse' their consumers by extending beyond the initial product category.

Real-world branding

Unfortunately, the real world has moved on and these two assumptions no longer hold true. Nowadays, we live in a whole world of brands that stretch well beyond FMCG and furthermore most of these brands offer multiple products or services under the one brand name. Indeed, many brands now offer both products and services.

The use of branding has expanded. Branding is now applied to services, retailers, corporations, not-for-profit organizations, digital enterprises, destinations, pop stars and even you and me through the notion of personal branding.

No longer is the world of branding confined to products like Coca-Cola, Volkswagen and Guinness; it now encompasses service brands like British Airways, HSBC and Vodafone. Corporate and business-to-business brands like Linklaters, Accenture and Boston Scientific exist alongside the not-for-profit brands like WWF, Médecins Sans Frontières and UNICEF.

Branding has also stretched into country or destination branding, with brands for England, Jamaica, New Zealand and just about every other country and region in the world. Sports brands include the likes of Manchester United and Real Madrid, and celebrity branding is a major industry in its own right, with the likes of David Beckham and Kim Kardashian. The successful relaunch of the Labour Party in the mid 1990s as New Labour was universally described as a rebrand, showing just how important marketing and branding is in politics too.

Digital brands have burst onto the scene in recent years, such as Amazon, Uber, threadless and Expedia.

FMCGs are no longer the heartland of branding. For many years Coca-Cola was rated as the world's most valuable brand according to the annual Interbrand 'Best brands' survey, but in 2016 it was only number 3[4] and in other brand valuation lists it was even lower: number 11 in the Brand Finance survey[5] and number 13 in the Brandz list.[6]

The brands that now dominate these lists are brands that offer a range of products and services, brands like Apple, Microsoft, Amazon and BMW. This is a demonstration that the so-called 'trap of line extension' no longer holds, if it ever did. Few brands, especially larger ones, are single product or single service brands any more. Instead, they provide a portfolio of offers, products and services or sometimes both.

In a world where creating new brands is still often seen as high risk, '9 out of 10 new brands fail don't they?', brand and line extensions seems a better, safer and potentially cheaper option for driving brand growth. Leveraging your existing brand equity to introduce new line extensions; new varieties, flavours, sizes and/or stretching your brand into new sectors, or indeed completely new markets, has become the name of the game and despite the examples quoted by Ries and Trout, there are now many, many more examples of successful line extensions.

Of course, some extensions still fail. Marketing isn't a pure science with rigid laws; some marketers get things wrong with extensions but many more consistently get things right.

Mars was for a long time essentially a one-product brand – a confectionery bar made of 'the goodness of milk, sugar, glucose and thick, thick chocolate...' as they said in their ads for many years. Nowadays, however, you can buy Mars bars in a variety of sizes; you can get Mars drinks, ice creams, chilled desserts, cakes and biscuits.

There are lots of examples of successful extensions that predate Ries and Trout's book and their concerns about the practice. One very famous brand extension opened its doors for the first time on 17 July 1955, four days after the founder's 30th wedding anniversary, and according to the original brochure was designed to be 'a place for people to find happiness and wonder'.

By 1950, Disney had already extended from its base in animated films into live action films and from there they moved into television creating successful series like *Davy Crockett* and *Zorro and Son*. In 1954, in what was to be a bold move, Disney bought land in the farming community of Anaheim, about 25 miles southeast of Los Angeles, and began construction on a US $17 million amusement park.

Today, Disneyland hosts more than 14 million visitors a year, who spend close to US $3 billion. Disney is nowadays a hugely extended brand doing everything from clothes to cruises, from toys to theme parks, from children's TV channels to video games. In fact, Disney also built its own town. The town of Celebration in Florida is perhaps the ultimate brand extension, allowing you not only to go on holiday to Disney but also to live the Disney life full time!

Think of Cadbury, which began life in tea, coffee and drinking chocolate and should, according to Ries and Trout, focus on confectionery but now stretches into biscuits, cakes, chilled desserts, ice creams, cereal bars and even an alcoholic chocolate liqueur.

More recently, if Apple had followed Ries and Trout's recommendations it wouldn't have extended beyond computers. It wouldn't have launched the iPod or the iPhone or their watches under the Apple name. Apple was rated the world's most valuable brand according to Forbes' 2016 list[7] and number 1 in Interbrand's 2016 list of the top 100 most valuable brands.[8] It wouldn't have got there without brand extension.

You can still buy Harley Davidson motorbikes but you can also smell like one too with their aftershave and eat in a Harley Davidson café. Even though I'm not sure I want to smell like a HOG (a member of the Harley Owners Group) it does demonstrate that brands are bigger than individual products.

Even Procter & Gamble, who for years seemed to follow the Ries and Trout 'don't extend' mantra, have now succumbed and realized significant benefits from line and brand extensions. Ivory is no longer just a soap; it's now a detergent and a washing-up liquid too. Mr Clean is a whole range of cleaners, liquids, sprays, wipes and erasers. Pampers offers nappies, nappy pants and wet wipes.

Nowadays, it is almost harder to think of a brand that has not been extended than to think of one that has.

In fact, in recent years P&G along with L'Oréal, Cadbury and Unilever and a number of other multinational companies announced their strategic intention to focus on a smaller number of brands. However, this isn't to restrict growth but to focus it. They aim to build the portfolios of product and services under each of their key brands. They want fewer bigger brands:

'P&G principal brands are down to 60. Its top 10 brands provide 50% of sales.'[9]

'L'Oreal has concentrated its efforts on ten major global brands which are responsible for 87% of cosmetics sales.'[10]

Danone has rationalized its portfolio of brands around health, selling off a raft of companies and brands including Panzani, Marie Surgeles, Kronenbourg, Galbani and HP Food.[11]

Virgin territory

However, perhaps the most cited brand that breaks the one-product rule is Virgin. Virgin is the antithesis of a one-product brand and, at times, its diversity has surprised and even confused the marketing world and its trade press.

If you look back over the first 30 years of the brand, you can see why.

1966 – A young Richard Branson founds a student magazine with a school friend.

1970 – He starts a mail order music business.

1971 – Branson opens his first shop.

1973 – The original Virgin logo is developed and registered; Virgin Records releases its first albums including the best-selling *Tubular Bells* by Mike Oldfield.

1977 – Virgin signs the Sex Pistols.

1984 – Having sold a major stake in Virgin Music, Branson uses some of his capital and launches Virgin Airline to the surprise of most of the recording and airline worlds.

1985 – Virgin Holidays is formed and many in the marketing world believe Branson has just changed track from music to holidays.

1993 – Virgin Radio is launched – is this a return to his roots?

1994 – In a move that stunned and appalled the marketing fraternity, Virgin Cola is launched taking on the mighty Coca-Cola.

1995 – In what seemed an opportunistic move, Virgin Vodka launches.

1996 – The move that generated more marketing press debate than any other: Branson launches Virgin Personal Finance. Then, later that year, if finance wasn't enough Virgin Internet and Virgin Brides are both launched.

It is at this point, if not even earlier that many are starting to ask: 'What is the Virgin brand?' It didn't and still doesn't seem to conform to the old brand models.

What is Virgin?

- A record company?
- A cola?
- A vodka?
- An airline?
- A train company?
- A media company?
- A financial institution?

Richard Branson answered the question in an interview he gave to *Marketing Week* in 1994: 'There is little to hold them together except the Virgin brand, but we do have the brand and we can license it to a diverse group of interests.'[12]

The Virgin brand is not tied to any one product or service or indeed one category; it is an entity that can be applied across categories. The brand philosophy is about being an anti-establishment consumer champion, taking on the 'big, bad boys' in a category and offering its consumers a better deal. He has described it himself: 'It's about taking on big conglomerates and moving into their territory and seeing if we can shake them up.'[13]

It is based around a set of beliefs and principles that Branson and his team have consistently spoken about:

- Business can be a force for good.
- Someone needs to stand up for the little guy.
- To do business as if there is a tomorrow.
- To recognize that staff matter most.

In other words, Virgin could be seen as an alternative model of branding to the traditional one included earlier in the chapter. It stands the traditional model of a 'product plus' on its head. It suggests that rather than starting with a product or service and adding a name, identity, a set of values and a specific proposition to it, you can start with the brand itself.

The first stage in this model of brand building is all about the brand definition, the purpose, the philosophy and the personality, and then and only then do you need to work out how and where it can be applied, into what product or service categories (see Figure 2.2).

Figure 2.2   An alternative brand-led model of brand development

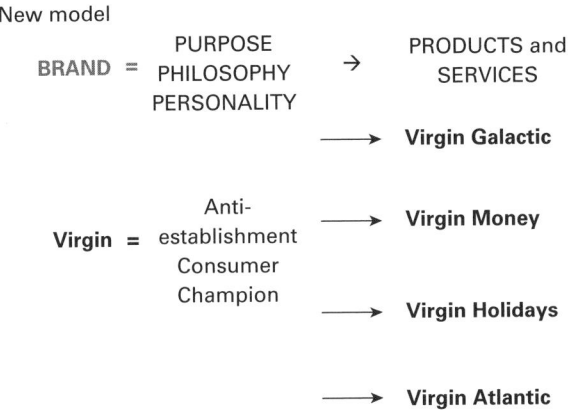

In Virgin's case this meant taking on big conglomerates, like British Airways, the high street banks and the traditional holiday companies, and trying to shake them up.

This 'model' may be slightly overstating the case. The idea of an alternative model, which completely reverses the previous one, is appealing but it probably stretches the truth a bit. Most brands do have to start somewhere doing something specific. So, perhaps a more realistic interpretation is a third model of brand development that is a combination of the traditional approach and the alternative new model (see Figure 2.3).

Here, the first manifestation of the brand is built with the first product (or service) as in the traditional model, but as soon as the brand is established in a way that takes it beyond that product (or service) then the brand owner can look at how it can be applied in

Figure 2.3   A model combining the traditional 'product plus' model and the alternative brand-led model showing a more realistic explanation of how modern brands extend

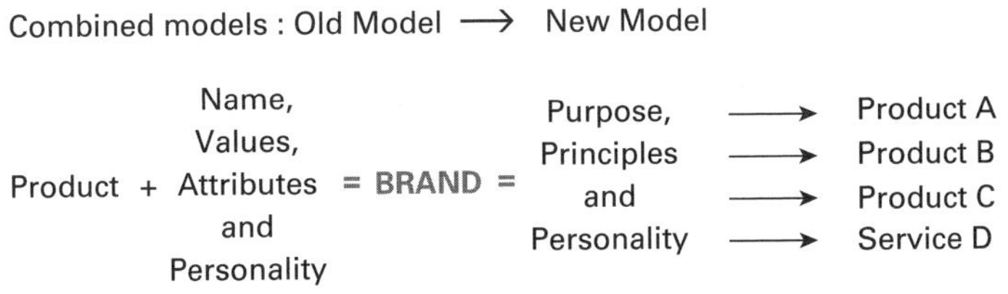

Combined models : Old Model ⟶ New Model

Name,
Values,
Product + Attributes = BRAND =
and
Personality

Purpose, ⟶ Product A
Principles ⟶ Product B
and   ⟶ Product C
Personality ⟶ Service D

other markets with other products and services. The brand then has the freedom to behave in the way shown in the second model.

As Will Whitehorn, Corporate Affairs Director, has said: 'The [Virgin] brand transcends any one product.'[14]

This model reflects the reality of many modern brands, which start life as a single product, service or even a range in one category but once they have established a clear brand positioning (of values, attributes and personality), they are leveraged to take the brand into new markets.

What this also demonstrates is that positioning in practice has evolved from being more product/category related, in the way Ries and Trout originally described it, to becoming less product specific and much broader and more conceptual.

The core Walt Disney brand, for example, is not about films but the wonderful, magical world of family entertainment. Microsoft is about fulfilling your potential. Dove is about championing female self-confidence and real beauty for real women.

As will be discussed in later chapters, there is still a need for more product or service focused go-to-market propositions but that these are different from the more conceptual, philosophical notion of branding, where a brand isn't just a name or just a single product. A brand is likely to encompass a number of products and services, and each of these may well need their own proposition.

Internal branding – looking in as well as out

As noted above, the Virgin brand core beliefs include the idea that staff matter most. In a world where, as will be discussed later, the customer is often seen as king, Sir Richard Branson says they should come second.

On the Virgin website he explains:

'Learn to look after your staff first and the rest will follow. Customer service can make or break a business. If you treat your staff well, they will be happy. Happy staff are proud staff, and proud staff deliver excellent customer service, which drives business success.'[15]

He explains that staff come first, customers second and shareholders third because getting the first two right will deliver the returns the shareholders want.

What this highlights is another area into which brands have moved, namely 'internal' branding. Originally, brands were seen as the public face of a company or a product, directed at its customers. This, too, has changed and nowadays brands are recognized as having a significant role 'internally'. As many commentators now point out 'the best brands come from within'.

'Internal' branding is seen as key to defining the culture and service style of a company or brand. In other words, branding also helps define and shape how a company or brand and its people should perform. This reflects the understanding that branding isn't just about what you offer (physically) but the way and the style in which you deliver that offer. It's no longer just what you do but the way that you do it. It's about the brand's culture and service philosophy.

In their book *Built to Last*, first published in 1994, Porras and Collins identify a strong and clearly defined culture as one of a number of defining characteristics of really successful companies (brands). Companies they define as 'visionary'. In fact, they go as far as to say that they have 'cult-like' cultures, by which they mean:

> 'something much stronger than just culture at work. "Cult-ism" and
> "cult-like" are descriptive – not pejorative or prescriptive – terms to
> capture a set of practices that we saw more consistently in the visionary
> companies than the comparison companies.'[16]

While wary of the comparison with extreme cults, they do say:

> 'the visionary companies translate their ideologies into tangible mecha-
> nisms aligned to send a consistent set of reinforcing signals. They
> indoctrinate people, impose tightness of fit, and create a sense of belong-
> ing to something special.' [17]

The language may have changed but the notion of defining and embedding a core ideology – or brand philosophy – is now well recognized and a goal for most companies. Employers know that their brand and its ideology can play a role in the recruitment and retention of employees:

- Surveys have shown that potential employees have a desire to work for an employer whose values mirror theirs.
- They look for organizations that will add value to their CVs and future employment prospects.
- Internal culture can play an important role in staff retention.

Brand image and reputation can play a big part in employment decisions, sometimes even more prominent than pay, in their choice of work. Nowadays, all Honda staff are given a corporate handbook when they join the company. *The Book of Everything* contains the usual company handbook information but more notably it has extensive sections on the Honda brand philosophy.

New Disney employees – or rather cast members in Disney's terms – attend the Disney University to be schooled in the ways and beliefs of the brand and their approach to guest service. Everybody goes, including senior management, and as Michael Eisner recalls in Doug Lipp's book *Disney U: How Disney University develops the world's most engaged, loyal and customer-centric employees*:

> 'When I first arrived at The Walt Disney Company, I was surprised to find I had to go back to school—at Disney University! There, I learned the fundamentals of guest service that consistently gave Disney a tremendous advantage in the marketplace.'[18]

Employees, whether existing employees or potential new recruits, are therefore another target audience for the brand, a target audience with its own perception of the brand, its own needs and motivations.

CASE STUDY

The Nordstrom story is perhaps one of the most famous examples and has been told a number of times: I wrote a version of it for my book – *The Prisoner and The Penguin*.

A tired old story?

A middle-aged man is wheeling a tyre (or as this story takes place in America it's probably fairer to say a 'tire') up and down outside a Nordstrom store in

Fairbanks, Alaska. He keeps stopping and peering in through the window. He looks a bit confused. Soon he starts to walk up and down again.

Finally, after a few minutes he comes in to the Nordstrom store, and wheels the tire up to one of the cash desks. There the clerk says a bright 'Good morning' to him; 'Can I help you?'

Meanwhile, and completely unbeknown to the clerk, standing in the background are John Nordstrom, a member of the store's founding family and the store manager. They are both watching with interest.

'I hope so,' says the man, a little bit embarrassed. 'I bought these tires in this store, never got round to fitting them and don't need them anymore. I was hoping to return them.'

Now, this is a Nordstrom store, part of a chain of department stores that sells a wide range of men's and ladies' fashion but not automotive products, and certainly not tires. Despite this, the clerk asks, 'Do you have a receipt?'

'I'm afraid not,' answers the man.

'Well, can you remember how much it cost?'

'I think it was about $25.'

'OK,' says the clerk and opens up his till. He takes out $25 and hands them over to the man, who smiles, thanks the clerk and leaves the store.

John Nordstrom and the store manager look at each other and walk straight over to the clerk and say...

'Well done.'

Now, being praised by your senior management for giving a refund on a product that your company doesn't even sell may seem a little strange, but then there is a little bit more to the story, and a lot more to Nordstrom's approach to customer service.

The 'little more' to the story is that the man may have been confused because the particular Nordstrom store was one of three stores that had previously been owned and run by NCC (Northern Commercial Company) and were sold to Nordstrom. NCC operated department stores too, but they also operated auto-dealerships and tire centers so the man may well have bought some tires from them.

The 'lot more' is that Nordstrom has, since it began in 1901, prided itself on its customer service and has become almost synonymous with it. It has a liberal, no quibble returns policy. Those looking to return goods are not challenged to produce receipts for goods that are clearly Nordstrom stock. Sales staff are known to deliver special orders personally to customers' homes. They are universally knowledgeable and courteous. They genuinely seem to want to help customers.

And behind this sits one of the most interesting employee handbooks in the world. It reads (in its entirety):

EMPLOYEE HANDOOK

Welcome to Nordstrom. We're glad you're here.

Our number one goal is to provide outstanding customer service. Set both your personal and professional goals high. We have great confidence in your ability to achieve them, so our employee handbook is very simple. We have only one rule...

OUR ONE RULE

Use good judgement in all situations.

Please feel free to ask your department manager, store manager or Human Resources officer any question at any time.

And that's it.

A quick footnote to the story: The tire story is a well-known tale and part of Nordstrom's folklore. There is some debate as to whether or not it is true. However, what I can personally confirm is true is the existence of the handbook and its exact contents. I wrote to Nordstrom and politely asked if the handbook that I had first heard about many years ago still existed.

I received a personal letter back from Jamie Nordstrom, President, Nordstrom Direct, in which he says the employee handbook, which is in fact an A5 card: 'continues to be a part of our culture. Our new employees receive the card on the first day of training.'[19]

He kindly enclosed a copy of the card. It still makes me smile when I compare it with other more weighty employee handbooks I have seen, but as an example of how branding works inside out it is one of the best.

The media revolution

If the brandscape has changed significantly in the last 35 years, the media world and brand communications have undergone a complete revolution.

It is sometimes hard for many under the age of 35 to grasp the scale of transformation. The UK got its fourth TV channel at 4.45 pm on 2 November 1982. Soon there will be millions of different channels and you will require new forms of search engine to help you find what you want.

In 1982, a list of every person who had an e-mail address fitted in to one small directory – the ARPANET (Advanced Research Projects

Agency Network) Directory. Danny Hillis, the man who registered the third domain name on the internet, brought one of these directories on stage with him in his talk, given at TED2013. Hillis said that the size and weight of the book makes the online community of the time seem 'deceptively large'.

> 'There's actually only about 20 people on each page — because we have the name, address and telephone number of each person, and everyone's listed twice because they're there once by name and once by email address... There were only two other Dannys on the internet then. I knew them both.'[20]

Google was only launched in 1998. Social media hadn't even been invented then. Facebook, LinkedIn, Twitter, WhatsApp and Instagram are all 21st-century brands.

What was large back in the 1980s were mobile phones. First commercially introduced in 1983, the Motorola DynaTac 8000X weighed two pounds, was the size of a brick, had a battery that would give you 35 minutes' talk time, took 10 hours to recharge and cost US $3,995.

Media usage is growing so rapidly (see Table 2.1) that if I tried to list a set of figures for it, the list would be out of date by the time this book is published. Needless to say, the opportunities for brands to engage with different sets of people have consequentially grown exponentially and are still growing.

Table 2.1 The Media Revolution

Year	Technology	Brand
1982	Instant messaging The compact disc	Channel 4 (UK)
1985		Windows Internet of things (term first used)
1990	World Wide Web	
1992	SMS	
1993	DVDs	Wired magazine
1994	Banner ads	The Electronic Telegraph – UK first online newspaper Sony Playstation

(continued)

Table 2.1   *(Continued)*

Year	Technology	Brand
1995		Amazon
		Monster
1997	Blogging	Netflix
		Channel 5
1998	Blu-Ray	Backrub becomes Google
1999	DVRs	Craiglist
		Blogger
2000	QR codes	AOL merges with time Warner
	.biz, .info, .name, .pro, .museum, .aero and .coop	
	USB sticks	
2001	Satellite radio	Wikipedia
		X-Box
		Napster (comes and goes)
		iPod
2002		Friendster
		LinkedIn
2003	RSS feeds	MySpace
	Mobile blogging	Skype
2004	Podcasting	Facebook
	Web 2.0	Flickr
2005		YouTube
		iTunes stores
		BBM Blackberry Messenger
2006		Twitter
		Nintendo Wii
		Google buys YouTube
2007		iPhone
		Netflix streaming
		BBC iPlayer
		Soundcloud
		Amazon Kindle

(continued)

Table 2.1   *(Continued)*

Year	Technology	Brand
2008	Online television	White House first post Google Chrome Spotify Amazon moves into film production
2010		Instagram
2011		Snapchat
2013		Netflix moves into content creation Google Glass
2015		WhatsApp

Not only has the sheer amount of communication changed radically, the style has or is also changing dramatically. Brand communication is moving from being predominantly unidirectional 'interruption' advertising to multichannel, multi-touchpoint customer experience and engagement marketing dialogues. We have moved from interruption to content marketing in media.

As Javier Sánchez Lamelas says in his book *M-ART-keting: The heart and the brain of branding*:

> 'This is a massive change as the vast majority of today's marketing is based on interruption. The original idea rested on the fact that people tolerated bad content (advertising interruption) in exchange for great content (sports, series, movies, news and so on). However, as people get control of *what, when and how* they consume content, the interruption model will lose its effectiveness. People will not tolerate bad content.'[21]

The drive for better marketing content has led to a change not just in means of engaging customers but the tone with which it is done. When the world was recovering from the Second World War and associated shortages of just about every product in the 1950s, brand owners often acted as the 'adults' talking down to their consumers as 'children' telling them about the virtues of their products. At times, they almost seemed to suggest that consumers were lucky to be offered the opportunity to buy the brand. It was a one-way sell (Figure 2.4).

Over time this has changed. As economies and wealth have grown, as competition increased, as media channels proliferated and consumers' media and marketing literacy grew there was more resistance to the sometimes patronizing tone of voice.

As universal social media established itself, as people have gained more control of what they wanted by either paying to get interruption-free media, like Netflix, or by getting software to do the job for them, brands realized that the conversations between brand and consumer needed to become more and more two-way or indeed social conversations. These conversations are now much more 'adult-to-adult' in nature, reflecting a more equal relationship where both parties treat each other with respect.

Conversations and dialogue are two-way and the internet and social media have not only provided people with a means of easily conversing with the brand, they have also created the opportunity for user-generated content on a huge scale. Marketing conversations

Figure 2.4 One-way adult-to-child communication

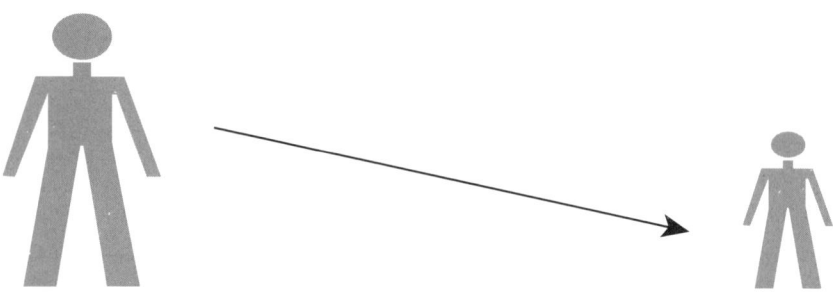

Figure 2.5 Two-way adult-to-adult conversation

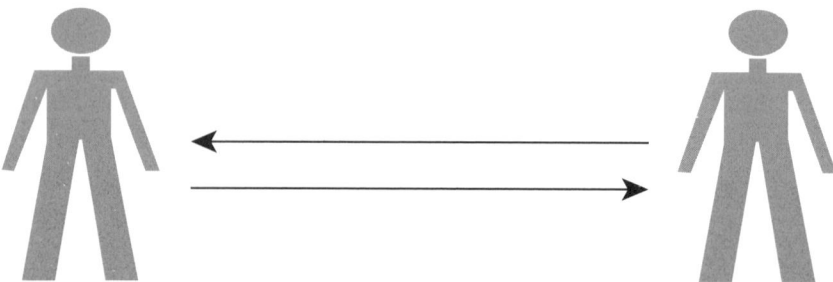

have become not just two-way but multiway and no longer do brands have total control (Figure 2.5).

(In fact, in Chapter 3 we will see how the pendulum may have swung even further in the direction of the 'little consumer' to such an extent that now they are 'royalty' and in control.)

In conclusion

To summarize this chapter, the world of brands – the brandscape – has fundamentally changed in the last 30 years. The new reality is that today's brands operate in a chaotic, ever-changing, multimedia, multi-customer world.

Branding has spread from the world of FMCG to just about every avenue of life, from services to superstars, from the external face of an organization to the culture within.

Brand extension is now the norm not the exception. It is a proven means of successful growth. Brands are therefore crossing boundaries of category, country and audience. They therefore have to talk about different things to different people, in different ways across different channels, all without appearing to have some form of multiple personality disorder or schizophrenia.

If the world of brands has changed significantly in the last 30 years, the media world is almost unrecognizable. Multiple channels, the web and smartphones are the norm. Mobile phones were just appearing on the scene in the early 1980s; they are now one of life's essentials with people in group discussions claiming 'I'd rather lose my wallet than my phone'.

Changes in media also mean that the old interruption model of marketing is rapidly fading and new models of engagement, user-generated content, are shaping the future of branding.

All of which means that we live in, if anything, an even more 'over-communicated society' than the one first described by Ries and Trout. However, this does raise the question as to whether a single 'over-simplified message' is likely to work across all the different groups a brand is targeting. Does one size fit all?

With more marketing- and media-literate consumers, will an over-simplified model be engaging enough on an ongoing basis to build the sorts of relationships marketers want for their brands nowadays? We are already seeing the demand for better content: content that people want to watch and not skip or ignore.

The challenge for brands will be to provide the greater depth and variety that will need to engage and hold different people's interest, all the while remaining true to the brand's purpose and philosophy.

The brandscape has changed, so now the language and thinking about branding needs to change too.

Notes

1   Perry, M (1996) 'Sunlight Soap', transcript, *Advertising Association of Great Britain*, Speech

2   Kotler, P and Keller, K (2015) *Marketing Management*, 15th edn, Pearson, London

3   Brand (2013) In: *Collins Concise English Dictionary*, 8th edn, Collins, London

4   Interbrand (2017) [accessed 10 January 2017] Best Brands, *Interbrand* [Online] http://interbrand.com/best-brands/best-global-brands/2016/ranking/

5   Brand Finance (2016) [accessed 16 January 2017] Global 500 2016: The annual report on the world's most valuable brands [Online] http://brandfinance.com/knowledge-centre/reports/brand-finance-global-500-2016/

6   Wppbaz.com (2016) *Brandz* [Online] http://wppbaz.com/charting/19

7   Forbes (2016) [accessed 10 January 2017] The World's Most Valuable Brands [Online] http://www.forbes.com/powerful-brands/list/#tab:rank

8   Interbrand (2017) [accessed 10 January 2017] Best Brands, *Interbrand* [Online] http://interbrand.com/best-brands/best-global-brands/2016/ranking/

9   Nurmalya Kumar (2003) [accessed 10 January 2017] Kill a Brand, Keep a Customer, *Harvard Business Review,* December 2003 [Online] https://hbr.org/2003/12/kill-a-brand-keep-a-customer

10 L'OREAL ANNUAL REPORT (2011) [Online] Available at: http://
loreal-dam-front-resources-corp-en-cdn.brainsonic.com/ressources/
afile/2539-30db6-resource-l-oreal-2011-activity-report.html
[accessed 10 January 2017].

11 Brandgym (2016) [accessed 27 January 2017] Four ways to focus
your brand portfolio [Blog] *The Brand Gym Blog* [Online] http://
wheresthesausage.typepad.com/my_weblog/2016/06/ways-to-focus-
your-brand-portfolio.html

12 Interview with Richard Branson (1994) *Marketing Week*

13 Interview with Richard Branson (1994) *Marketing Week*

14 Dwek, R (1996) [accessed 10 January 2017] Top UK Brands and
Clients: How far can brand extensions be pushed? *Campaign* [Online]
http://www.campaignlive.co.uk/article/top-uk-brands-clients-far-brand-
extensions-pushed/28372

15 Virgin (2017) [accessed 10 January 2017] Staff come first [Online]
https://www.virgin.com/richard-branson/staff-come-first

16 Collins, J and Porras, J (2002) *Built to Last*, Collins Business
Essentials, New York

17 Collins, J and Porras, J (2002) *Built to Last*, Collins Business
Essentials, New York

18 Lipp, D (2013) *Disney U: How Disney University develops the world's
most engaged, loyal and customer-centric employees* 1st edn, McGraw-
Hill Education, USA

19 Jamie Nordstrom (no date) Employee handbook, Nordstrom Direct,
Cedar Rapids, Iowa

20 Hillis, D (2013) [accessed 27 January 2017] The Internet could
crash.We need a Plan B. In: TED conference, New York, *TED2013*
[Online]https://www.ted.com/talks/danny_hillis_the_internet_
could_crash_we_need_a_plan_b

21 Sánchez Lamelas, J (2016) *Martketing: The heart and brain of
branding*, 1st edn, LID Publishing, London

An abdication of responsibility

The abdication of Belief
Makes the Behavior small
Better an ignis fatuus
Than no illume at all.
EMILY DICKINSON[1]

Long live the King

At a time when the marketing world has never been more complex and the drive for simplification has never been greater, what are brand owners doing to reconcile these apparently polar opposites?

Well, it seems some are clinging to outdated thinking while others are in danger of abdicating their responsibilities for their brands. They are handing over the reins to their consumers and customers; in fact, to anyone and everyone who has a perception of their brand.

'The customer is king' now seems to be a cornerstone of modern branding, and brand owners appear to be rushing to hand over their crown jewels – their brands. One manifestation of this is the emergence of the CCO – the Chief Customer Officer, described in his article for the *Harvard Business Review* by Paul Hagen:

> 'The customer's voice has a new champion sitting at the highest levels
> of power in companies. Whether firms call the position Chief Customer
> Officer (CCO) or some other label, these individuals serve as top executives
> with the mandate and power to design, orchestrate, and improve customer
> experiences across the ever-more-complex range of customer interac-
> tions. The role exists in B2B and B2C firms as diverse as Allstate, Dunkin'
> Brands, USAA, Philips Electronics, FedEx, the Cleveland Clinic, and SAP.'[2]

The argument in favour of this transfer of power to customers seems to have two main threads:

Firstly, and perhaps most importantly, is the idea that as the true value of brands lies in customers' perceptions of them and as these perceptions rest in the individual customers' minds, it is the customers – not the manufacturers or trademark proprietors – who 'own' the brands. In arguments advocating this approach you often see phrases like: 'A customer's perception is their reality'.

The second thread is that brands are often shaped by factors and actions that are beyond those in their control. An oft-quoted example is a much-publicized photo of Daniella Westbrook, the infamous ex-star of television soap opera *Eastenders*. *The Scotsman* mentions the following in late 2003:

> 'Burberry has "jumped the shark". The US term, coined to describe the exact point at which a successful television programme suddenly dips towards mediocrity, is equally applicable to clothes lines.
>
> Just as the audience for *Happy Days* never enjoyed the antics of the Fonz in the same way after he leapt a glass tank containing a live shark, so admirers of Burberry's trademark check sighed and slung it to the back of the wardrobe after Daniella Westbrook, a self-confessed addict, publicly overdosed on Burberry.
>
> The image of Westbrook in a Burberry skirt and Burberry jacket hauling a Burberry-clad baby out of a Burberry wrapped buggie was the point at which the label's marketing men could be forgiven for slapping their foreheads and crying: "D'Oh!".'[3]

In addition, as Javier Sánchez Lamelas notes in his book *M-ART-keting*, for some marketers the changes in the media world, namely the 'combination of media proliferation and user-generated content makes it virtually impossible to give brands direction'.[4]

He goes on to reflect that many marketers who believe this think that they should follow this trend and let people do what they want with the brand.

To take this to its logical conclusion, if the customer is now king and owns the brand then the concept of brand ownership has been stood on its head. From its origin as a mark of personal ownership, this interpretation gives ownership to the many. Like Javier Sánchez Lamelas, I believe this is 'lazy marketing'.[5]

A half-truth becomes whole

I believe that the origins of this transfer of ownership can be traced back to a specific occasion: a British Brands Group lecture given by Jeremy Bullmore on 5 December 2001. As a former Chairman of both J Walter Thompson and the Advertising Association, and still currently a director at the WPP Group, his words carry a lot of weight.

In his presentation, he argued that brands are in part reliant on their fame and that this fame resides in the minds of members of the public and customers who have become aware of brands. He went on to suggest that these perceptions of brand celebrity vary as much as those who perceive them, as each individual has their own personal and unique view of a brand.

Bullmore's aim was to highlight the importance and power of customers – and, indeed, other factors beyond marketers' control – in shaping a brand's positioning and in shaping the destiny of brands generally.

He was highlighting the difficulties and intricacies of brand stewardship, partly as an explanation of why brands are so difficult to value financially. Bullmore built a compelling argument as he said that: 'brands are fiendishly complicated, elusive, slippery, half-real/half-virtual things.'[6]

However, he also went on to say that: 'the image of the brand – its brand reputation – that which makes it the shareholders' most valuable asset – doesn't belong to it. It belongs to those who give thought to it.'[7]

He was in essence transferring ownership from the traditional brand owner and/or shareholder to the general public. It is this contention, which was actually about the 'ownership' of a brand's reputation and not the actual brand ownership, that has been twisted and is now being spouted as the whole and gospel truth by a large number of marketers.

Bullmore himself noted:

> 'For the sake of economy, and to some extent for effect, I have made some half-truths into whole truths and presented them more starkly than perhaps a more conscientious lecturer would have ventured to do.'[8]

My concern is that this is another example of oversimplification and too many marketers have heard the headline, this 'half-truth', and have started to repeat it without thinking it through and considering all the consequences. As noted earlier, we live in a world of sound-bites, and I am concerned that this one will bite marketers and brand owners if they are not careful.

There is no doubt about the importance of the customer, the notion of individual perception or the inability of companies to control all aspects of what will shape brand perception, but that doesn't mean that there isn't still a strong case for the old kings – the brand owners – to retain or if necessary reclaim ownership of their brands. The brand owners need to set and drive the direction of their brands.

Making the case for retaining ownership starts with a legal issue. I am no lawyer; however, even instinctively, the notion that a (marketing) director of a company that legally 'owns' a brand could publicly proclaim that they do not think they really 'own' that brand, seems patently dangerous to me. It seems illogical, as that self-same brand may be highly valued on the company's own balance sheet.

If companies do not 'own' their brands, how can they expect to defend their rights over that brand?

Giving up 'ownership' could have all sorts of unwanted consequences. If a brand owner uses its trademark – the legally registered sign for the brand – in a way that is liable to mislead the public, that trademark can be revoked. However, if it allows others to 'own' and use its trademark as they want there is a much greater likelihood of its use in ways that could mislead others.

Giving up ownership could also give a green light to counterfeiters to reproduce, replicate and trade-off brands. If challenged, the counterfeiters can simply refute any claims of damages. They will simply argue that, as the companies do not own the brands and they (the counterfeiters) along with everyone else do own them, then they have the right to reproduce them.

And it is worth noting that the counterfeiting of brands is already a major problem. The OECD reported that:

'Imports of counterfeit and pirated goods are worth nearly half a trillion dollars a year, or around 2.5% of global imports, with US, Italian and French brands the hardest hit and many of the proceeds going to organized crime, according to a new report by the OECD and the EU's Intellectual Property Office.'[9]

Returning to the notion of 'public ownership' and the argument around individual perceptions, it is worth stressing again that when this argument is made, it is referring to brand perceptions rather than the brand itself, or the trademark by which it is denoted.

Ownership and an enigmatic smile

So while it is undoubtedly true that we all have individual perceptions and experiences of the brands we know, and we can even feel like we 'own' at least a part of those brands, we don't really own the subject or brand in question. We don't legally own it; nor do we even fully control it.

As customers, we can influence the brand, and even control it to some extent by purchasing it, by using or not using it in public, by talking about it to friends, family or via social media and maybe even creating content for it. Our actions can and do have consequences. If everyone stops buying a certain brand, it is likely to go out of business. As such, we, its customers, are perhaps the most powerful influencing force or pressure group on that brand.

But we are not, and never will be, the owners. We can stop buying a brand, we can ignore it, we can suggest and influence alterations, but we do not actually enact those changes or have final control.

There is perhaps an interesting parallel with the *Mona Lisa*, which enjoys 'awareness' or fame in the way a brand does, and which engenders a wide range of different perceptions from everyone who has ever seen it. In other words, we each have perceptions of the painting in our mind, but it would seem foolish to suggest that any or all of us actually owns the *Mona Lisa*. All we own is our perception of the painting.

I believe it is vital that marketers continue to recognize the importance of the brand owners' role in 'owning' their brands. Individual perceptions are crucial, but branding is all about the creation and management of meaning en masse.

Branding is a social phenomenon. In fact, as we have seen, the origins of modern branding arose out of the Industrial Revolution and the development of mass production, which in turn drove the need to mark or brand one manufacturer's products to distinguish them from those of other traders.

The same revolution also led to the transformation of the economy from a rural one to an urban one, the mass population centres that were in the new industrial towns created places of mass consumption. Finally, the development of mass education provided the emerging brands with a mass audience that could consume (read) their mass communications – their packaging and advertising.

It is true that:

1 brand owners don't own the individual perceptions of brands that each and every one of us has;

2 some of the factors that create these perceptions are beyond the control of the brand owner; including the increasing amount of user-generated content;

3 these perceptions are organic in so far as they are created, evolve and change with time, events and experiences.

But, it is also true that brands are created as a 'mass' tool. Brands aren't about single transactions: they work in multiplicity, with many people, and on many occasions. For a brand, it's about mass understanding and mass recognition.

Brands as we have seen are a means by which their owners do their best to manage multiple relationships simultaneously. It is the role of the brand owner, through their brand, all its touchpoints and all the different brand encounters, to try to create and then manage the best perceptions of that brand.

The aim of marketers and brand owners is to create a positive, motivating and distinctive set of associations with their brand and to do so coherently among a large group of people. Individual perceptions can and will differ, but for strong brands there are a set of strong powerful associations. So when people see the famous Mercedes logo, they think 'car', 'German', 'premium', 'great engineering', 'comfortable' 'prestige' or maybe 'taxi'... When they see the Nike Swoosh, they think 'sports', 'attitude', 'Michael Jordan', 'trainers'.

It would be foolish to think that everyone will think exactly the same things, or that everyone will think positive things, about a brand (or even just one thing). But the aim of the brand owner is to create a set of positive associations and desirable expectations, which they then can successfully deliver (ideally) time and time again.

Brands can, therefore, be defined as a 'zip file' of meaning. The 'name' (or graphic representation) of the brand is a shorthand that, once accessed, unlocks or unzips a whole set of images, associations, feelings and memories.

And, indeed, by stretching the point a bit it could also be argued, as Immanuel Kant originally did in his *Copernican Revolution*, that it is the representation or brand identity that makes the object possible, rather than the object that makes the representation possible. It is therefore the brand owner who truly creates a brand when they give their product or service a representation (whether that's a name, icon or brand identity) and it is thereby the brand owner who establishes ownership of it.

One point on which I wholeheartedly agree with Jeremy Bullmore is that branding is not, and is unlikely ever to be, a science. If anything, it is closer to a social science, and it is in trying to create and manage brand as a successful social entity that the skill of a good marketer comes in. It is a mix of art and science and when it is done well, a brand creates a mass 'meaning' that is broadly coherent across different stakeholder groups and becomes a unit of social currency.

For example, there is a general understanding of exactly what is meant when phrases like 'bloody BMW drivers' or 'he's a *Guardian* reader' are used. We may all have individual perceptions of these brands but we also know the general agreed characteristics and meaning of those brands.

Hence, Sir Michael Perry, when Chairman of Unilever, said:

'In the modern world brands are a key part of how individuals define themselves and their relationships with one another... More and more we are simply consumers... We are what we wear, what we eat, what we drive.'[10]

UK fashion designer Jasper Conran defined and segmented women on the basis of their choice of fashion brand, using a technique that has been dubbed 'brandographics':

> 'There's the Versace woman who dresses for men, sans doubte. Versace girls make a career of sex; they don't have girlfriends, they're too much like competition. The Armani woman dresses for herself, and the Chanel woman dresses for other women. Chanel is all about branding; you know she's a woman who wants to make women envious.'[11]

Brandographics, like demographics and psychographics, is a method of segmenting and classifying people. However, as the name suggests, brandographics segments people according to the brands they buy and use. It is based on the idea that we express ourselves through the brands we select, so it is possible to build a profile of a person by understanding their choice of brands.

It rests, however, on the fact that brands, their meanings and associations are coherent and broadly consistent across the population and, despite individual differences in perception, are units of social currency. So, if I was to tell you I am a VW Beetle convertible driver, who likes to wear AX shirts and Jean-Paul Gaultier aftershave, who drinks Doom Bar and reads *The Guardian* you should be able to get at least a partial picture of what I am like.

That vision thing

As the best marketers know and accept, 'you can't please all of the people all the time'. Brands are also about choice. Customers making choices, employees making choices, investors making choices but also the brands themselves making choices. Choices about what they want to stand for, what they want to stand against.

Manchester United is one of the biggest and most valuable sports brands in the world and yet as many, if not more, people hate them than love them. Marmite, the yeast extract spread, has even made a virtue out of its polarized appeal, proudly proclaiming in its advertising that 'you either love us or hate us'!

While it is demonstrably true that customers apply a powerful force on brands, often influencing the brand's behaviour, it would potentially be very concerning if the general public, the customers were completely in charge. To paraphrase the late founder of Oglivy and Mather ad agency David Ogilvy, we consumers may not be 'morons'. We may be your wife, husband or partner, but we aren't always right.

Paraphrasing Steve Jobs: 'Sometimes we don't know what we want, or at least don't know until we are shown it'.[12]

Brand creation and extension are often the result of innovation, changing what already exists and/or creating new things. If the customers owned the brand and their word was final, then many, many brand innovations and the brands they would create would be killed before they were born. People are notoriously resistant to change and have often rejected ideas before they have seen or used them in practice.

While George H W Bush may famously not have been a fan of the need for an overarching vision, marketers need 'the vision thing'. That is, the belief that what you are doing is right, and that it should be done even if those around you don't always agree.

Without 'that vision thing' many of the great brand owners would not have created the brands they did. Walt Disney, W K Kellogg, Richard Branson, Phil Knight (the founder of Nike) and Anita Roddick (the founder of The Body Shop) wholeheartedly believed in what they were doing. They believed in creating something that existed in their minds long before it existed in the minds of what were often, at first, very dubious customers. They had the vision thing.

The idea of promoting a healthy diet based on grain seemed ridiculous at first, but that didn't stop W K Kellogg pursuing it. As the official Kellogg's website says:

'W. K. Kellogg was a man with a purpose ... to bring people the life-giving properties of grains in their most appetizing forms. He and his brother, Dr. John Harvey Kellogg, believed in and adhered to a food diet consisting largely of grains, nuts and fruits. At the Battle Creek Sanatorium (the San), where it was their job to provide patients with a nutritious diet, they experimented with corn, rice, wheat and oats to develop better tasting grain-based foods.'[13]

It is Walt Disney's beliefs, ideals and vision that are enshrined in the company that still bears his name. Walt Disney wanted to tell stories and still now, long after his death, employees ask themselves what would Uncle Walt do in relation to a new circumstance or opportunity?

Henry Ford might still be looking for a faster horse if he hadn't had the vision thing that allowed him to look at what the customers said they wanted.

CASE STUDY

Some decisions are only for the brave

1964 was a time of social turmoil and racial tension in the United States.

It was also the year of the World Fair, which was held in New York.

It would prove to be an important time in the history of SC Johnson which was, back then, only a comparatively small Wisconsin-based cleaning products manufacturer.

Herbert Fisk Johnson, the third generation SC Johnson leader, presented an idea to the board.

He suggested they build a Johnson Wax pavilion at the Fair in which they would screen a specially made film. It would use the firm's entire marketing budget on this prestigious but one-off event.

But that is not all: he didn't want the film to be about the company or any of its products, he wanted it to be about the simple joy of being alive. His vision was for a film designed to celebrate the common ground between different cultures by tracing how children in various parts of the world mature into adulthood. He wanted it to be a message of 'peace through understanding'. The film he proposed should be shot in various locations across the United States, Europe, Asia and Africa and feature a multiracial cast.

Not surprisingly, the other company executives weren't immediately enamoured with the idea. They had numerous questions and challenges.

After politely listening to all their concerns, HF thought for a while and then simply said: 'Some decisions are only for the brave.'

The 20-minute film was co-directed by Francis Thompson and Alexander Hammid and used an experimental method consisting of three separate 18-foot screens. Unlike the Cinerama process that joined three screens into a single unbroken entity, the three screens were separated by one foot of space.

To Be Alive! quickly became one of the fair's most popular exhibits. The public loved it. People lined up around the block to get a chance to see a screening.

Years later Fisk Johnson, HF's grandson recalled 'My grandfather, HF Johnson, Jr wanted to counter the negativity that was so apparent during this period of American history. He succeeded, bringing a new generation a message of hope and optimism.'

'It really put SC Johnson on the map… even though we didn't market our products at all,' says Kelly Semrau, SC Johnson's current head of sustainability.

Putting we, the customers, in charge would also lead to an ever-increasing reliance on market researchers asking us what we want. While I am a firm believer in the benefits of good market research, I also recognize its weaknesses. As Anita Roddick, one of those visionaries and not a research fan, said: 'Running a company on market research is like driving while looking in the rear view mirror.'[14]

Another weakness of a reliance on market research is that, as more and more brands decide to use market research to find the insights on which to build their brands, they all want to talk to us. They end up asking the same sort of people the same sorts of questions and all getting to the same answers at the same time. It's a recipe for bland-ness and not brand-ness, if we are not careful.

For example, if you wanted to create a new culinary aids brand you might ask people what they want from culinary aids. They will tell you exactly what they want from culinary aids in general – and if someone else asks them the same question they will say the same thing. There is a real danger everyone gets to the same answer.

The reason why I use this particular example is that I have read three brand visions for three culinary aids' brands, all based on the same customer insight. Each brand team has told me how good their vision is because it was customer-centric and based on a true customer understanding.

In conclusion

In this chapter, I have discussed how there has been a significant shift of power in the relationship between brand owners and us, the customers of their brands. We now live in a world where branding is an organic and a 'negotiated' unit of social and economic currency, and the concept of brandographics is one expression of this role for brands.

I go on to suggest that too many marketers are reacting to this shift by abdicating their responsibility and handing too much power to their customers, and that this is lazy and potentially dangerous marketing.

While agreeing that there are occasions where 'influence' over the brand can to a certain extent be taken away from the brand owner, I have argued that it is vital that the brand owner must recognize that they have ultimate control and ownership of their brand. I have highlighted a number of issues that could ensue from this abdication, both legal and marketing related. The danger of blandness and not brand-ness is paramount among these.

Building on this I highlight the importance of a brand having the vision thing and how it is the brand owners' responsibility to set the direction of the brand, change, or even withdraw their brand if they choose to do so. Brands may aim to help facilitate customer choices but they need to make their own choices first, what they stand for and what they stand against.

This notion of brand owners ultimately defining and controlling their brand based on the owners' vision, beliefs and principles is something that I will return to in later chapters as it is a key element in the construction of a purposeful brand philosophy.

Notes

1 Emily Dickinson [accessed 9 March 2017] Emily Dickinson Museum [Online] https://www.emilydickinsonmuseum.org/

2 Hagen, P (2011) [accessed 10 January 2017] The Rise of the Chief Customer Officer, *Harvard Business Review* [Online] https://hbr.org/2011/04/the-rise-of-the-chief-customer

3 *The Scotsman* (2003) [accessed 7 February 2017] Time for a Reality Check [Online] http://www.scotsman.com/lifestyle/time-for-a-reality-check-1-496482

4 Sánchez Lamelas, J (2016) *Martketing: The heart and the brain of branding*, 1st edn, LID Publishing, London

5 Sánchez Lamelas, J (2016) *Martketing: The heart and the brain of branding*, 1st edn, LID Publishing, London

6 Bullmore, J (2001) British Brands Group lecture

7 Bullmore, J (2001) British Brands Group lecture

8 Bullmore, J (2001) British Brands Group lecture

9 OECD/EUIPO (2016) *Trade in Counterfeit and Pirated Goods: Mapping the economic impact*, OECD Publishing, Paris

10 Perry, M (1996) Sunlight Soap, transcript, *Advertising Association of Great Britain*, Speech

11 Bruzzi, S and Gibson, P (2000) *Fashion Cultures*, 1st edn, Routledge, London

12 Bloomberg Businessweek (25 May 1998) [accessed 7 February 2017] *Steve Jobs* [Online] https://www.bloomberg.com/businessweek/1998/21/b3579165.htm (subscribers only) or quoted in Chunka Mui [accessed 31 May 2017] Five Dangerous Lessons to Learn From Steve Jobs, *Forbes* [Online] https://www.forbes.com/sites/chunkamui/2011/10/17/five-dangerous-lessons-to-learn-from-steve-jobs/#1754a7a93a95

13 Kellogg's (2017) [accessed 12 January 2017] Kellogg's UK: Breakfast cereals, healthy recipes and snacks [Online] http://www.kelloggs.co.uk/en_GB/home.html

14 Ridgers, B (2012) *The Economist Book of Business Quotations*, 1st edn, Economist, London

Proposition and positioning, marketing and branding

04

'In order to be irreplaceable one must always be different.'
COCO CHANEL

Fuzzy thinking

'What is the difference between a positioning and a proposition?'

I have been asked this question many times in my career, which in itself isn't perhaps surprising given that I've worked in marketing for 30 years. Perhaps what is more surprising is how senior the people asking it have been.

'What is the difference between branding and marketing?' is a question I often ask when interviewing candidates. My follow-up question is then, 'What's the difference between sales and marketing?' This is especially relevant in a world where marketing directors are increasingly judged on the latest short-term sales results.

What do all these questions tell us?

Other than 'curiosity is a required trait in marketers', they show that clear and consistent definitions of terms in branding are notoriously hard to find, with different companies, agencies and consultants all crafting their own particular twist. While this is understandable as they try to differentiate themselves one from another, it can lead to confusion, or as one marketing director described it to me: 'fuzzy thinking'.

In this chapter, I want to explore the difference between a proposition and a positioning, and define sales, marketing and branding independently and in relation to each other demonstrating the differences between them. One of the key implications of this will be to highlight the need for marketing to be customer-led, while branding needs 'the vision thing' discussed in Chapter 3. What this then suggests is that brands need to be customer-fed and not customer-led, an idea that reinforces the argument against brands being owned by the customer.

Time waits for no man... especially if he's a salesman

Sales are defined in most dictionaries in two ways: the exchange of a product, service or asset for money and the action of selling something. In the context of this discussion, this latter definition can perhaps be re-expressed as selling what your organization makes or delivers to a defined audience, in most cases with the aim of delivering a profit. It's about finding the offer they can't refuse – a compelling proposition that will close the deal and make your customer make that purchase.

Key to sales is therefore the proposition, which in turn can be defined as 'the offer of benefits made to a (specific) target audience that a brand promises it will deliver'. They are generally based on an (one) identified core target audience and an insight into that group's needs and motivations. Sales and propositions are therefore based in the here and now.

'Marketing is the management process responsible for identifying, anticipating and satisfying customer requirements profitably' is the definition of marketing used by the Chartered Institute of Marketing (CIM). Central to it is therefore an understanding of the current and future needs of your customers, and developing a way in which you can meet them, normally profitably. (Obviously, this doesn't hold true for charities and other not-for-profit organizations.)

Marketing includes activities like market research, advertising, communication and innovation. Marketing is therefore concerned with both the current and the future, though that future tends to have a relatively short-term perspective of three to five years.

Branding, I would suggest, is about having a purpose and a philosophy that uses appropriate marketing and sales to express those beliefs and so 'convert' people to it, again normally profitably, and over time. It is therefore about a long-term perspective.

One way, then, of differentiating between sales, marketing and branding is from this temporal point of view. Success in sales is often judged on performance in the last quarter or even last month, success for a marketing director is judged on a yearly or bi-annual basis (which may be why so many move on every 24 months), while success for a brand is often measured over decades or even centuries.

However, in recent years, there has been increasing pressure on marketing departments to demonstrate their value and their contribution to the business. Every CEO and CFO knows and will, at the first opportunity, wheel out William Hesketh Lever's famous quote about the uncertainty in the effectiveness of advertising: 'Half of my advertising is wasted, and the trouble is, I don't know which half.'[1] The CEOs and Financial Director and the shareholders don't like or want that waste.

In this environment, proven sales-generating marketing initiatives not surprisingly come to the fore and the net result is that in many instances marketing is becoming more sales orientated and more short term in its outlook. Marketing is now increasingly driven by the six months financial targets. Boardroom eyes are now firmly fixed on marketing and they are expecting it to deliver, and deliver promptly. ROI (return on investment) no longer just relates to capital expenditure, there are regular discussions about ROMI or return on marketing investment.

Speaking at Deloitte's Media and Telecoms conference in March 2017, the WPP boss, Sir Martin Sorrell, who at the time had a very young daughter, said: 'It's not three-month-old babies that keep me awake at night. It's the continuous focus on the short term.'[2]

When working recently with a medium-sized, publicly quoted company, owner of a number of famous brands, I was constantly told of stories how as soon as there was a danger of falling behind the figures quoted to the city, extra promotions would be added to their core brands to help deliver the necessary volumes. This wasn't happening just once or twice a year but increasingly regularly and the marketing team didn't feel that this was true marketing but just short-term sales generation.

They aren't the only company where this is the norm. Constant discounting is now a regular and ongoing feature in many markets where, over any given year, the majority of sales come when the brands are on offer. From tuna to wine, from sofas to telephone service suppliers, the majority of sales are driven by discounts and deals. A surprising number of markets are now price-promotion-led as marketing teams look for ways to ensure they deliver against those quarterly sales targets.

This continues in many markets, even though there is increasing evidence from the likes of Byron Sharp in *How Brands Grow* that promotions have little impact on long-term sales and brand growth. In fact, he suggests that the money put into promotions does little for the long-term brand and customer relationship but is at best an investment into the relationship the brands have with the retailers.

Constant discounting in the beer market by Stella Artois was felt to have been a factor that undermined its long-running 'Reassuringly Expensive' proposition and its premium positioning.

There are other, possibly less overt pressures on marketing to get closer to sales. For example, when it comes to marketing existing products and services, ones in which companies already have the technological infrastructure and supply chain and may have invested millions in them, then the difference between sales and marketing can really become a little blurred. There is huge self-interest and a strong profit incentive for those companies to sell more of what they can produce using their existing capabilities and resources.

Marketing and proposition development for those brands, and their products and services, is focused on identifying insights that drive the current business further. While incremental innovation utilizing existing capabilities is encouraged, significantly changing the product or service, the technology that delivers it, the supply lines or even changing market sector will involve significant investment and risk.

So, while innovation departments within those companies may explore how the customers' and consumers' needs can be better, differently or more cheaply met, the job of much of those brands' marketing departments will be on driving volume and value for the existing products and services whether that comes from share gains or increased category usage. In other words, marketing's job is too often to sell more of the specific product or service, and marketing in those instances is therefore close to sales and further from branding. It's all about developing the most compelling proposition..., which sounds remarkably close to the role of sales.

What's your position on positioning?

Positioning is a more complicated concept to define, partly because it is used in different ways and in many different contexts within marketing. There are, in fact, three main ways in which the term positioning is used:

1 market positioning;

2 needs positioning;

3 brand positioning.

Some of the confusion comes because, in common use, they are all referred to as simply 'positioning'.

The first use is 'market positioning', which includes, but isn't exclusively, price positioning. This application refers to assigning a brand to a sector of the market it sits in. What price partition is it in? Is it a super-premium, premium, mainstream or economy brand? What product sector is it in? Is it in the low calorie, full sugar or organic sector?

The second use is 'needs positioning', which refers to how a brand is positioned against consumer needs or where it is sited on a consumer needs map. For example, a brand of premium chocolate desserts would probably sit in the 'indulgent' needs sector, a range of large-sized ready meals in the 'gut-fill' sector and a reduced calories range would probably sit in the 'weight-management' sector. This sort of positioning can be done qualitatively by asking customers to 'map' the market, whereby they cluster products and are then asked to attribute role and 'needs' to each group, but more often it is done via a quantitative study, many of which have a standard bank of needs against which brands are positioned according to how consumers see them.

The third positioning application and the most relevant for this discussion is the notion of 'brand positioning'. As previously mentioned, still the most used definition is the one that comes from

Ries and Trout's book *Positioning*: 'a position in the prospect's mind, a position that takes into consideration not only a company's own strengths and weaknesses, but those of its competitors as well'.[3]

A brand positioning is therefore a summation of how the brand is perceived by the prospect, most often the core target group, what it offers those prospects and how the brand and its offer is differentiated from the competition.

The brand positioning and the model is a key point of reference for the marketing department, and for any brand planning. As has already been discussed, many of the current positioning models were built by marketing teams working with their advertising agencies, and therefore have often been used for the development of brand communications. As such, many are still built on the premise of a single product or service or at least a single target audience and the need to define the single most important thing to communicate.

As was seen in Chapter 1, these models have a specific section called 'brand proposition' along with others for target audience, consumer insight, reasons to believe, values, personality brand essence and differentiator. On one level, this identifies a key difference between a proposition and positioning. One, the proposition, is a subset of the other, the positioning.

However, it could perhaps equally be said that a brand positioning model is actually an expanded and fuller definition of the brand's core proposition. It can be said that this sort of brand positioning is centred on the core proposition but gives it context by including the target audience, the insight into their needs and motivations and more details on how that proposition should be expressed in keeping with its values and desired tone of voice. Whichever is the case, it is still an important tool for marketing – defining the way in which your brand should be taken to market. Given the importance of these documents, it is not surprising that thinking on brand positioning continues to evolve.

I have already talked about how the early focus on the USP broadened into the notion of (brand) positioning as defined by Ries and Trout in the 1980s, but it is possible to identify other iterations.

In the 1990s the communications agency, HHCL+Partners launched their manifesto and proclaimed: 'the USP is dead, long live the USP'.[4] They said that the old notion of Unique Selling Proposition should be confined to the bin and that in the future brands would need a Unique Selling Persona. They argued that the speed of technological development and the ensuing ease with which any product benefit, or the technology behind it, could be copied by competitors meant that any points of differentiation were likely to be short-lived. They argued that instead of focusing on product points of differentiation, brands should focus on developing a distinctive tone of voice and an accompanying way of acting – the unique selling persona.

HHCL developed an array of award-winning and business-driving brand campaigns around this philosophy, including most famously the 'You've been Tango'd' campaign. They were voted 'Agency of the Decade' by *Campaign* magazine in 2000.[5]

It can be argued that the main focus of their newly developed USPs were still on communication and go-to-market strategies. There was, however, a clear recognition of the importance of how a brand behaves and so, to some degree at least, this approach did start to encompass the notion of internal branding and its role in defining company culture.

More recently, we have seen the emergence of the brand purpose, which has led to further developments in the thinking about brand positioning. While in some ways, a brand purpose is a re-expression of the notion of a brand vision, it is one that reflects companies' realization of the societal role of brands.

Brand purpose has been variously defined as:

'a business's essential reason for being, the higher-order benefit it brings to the world'

Jim Stengel in *Grow*

'a reason "why" you exist beyond the desire to make profit'

On Purpose by Shaun Smith and Andy Milligan[6]

'an aspirational reason for being which inspires and provides a call to action for an organization and its partners and stakeholders and provides benefit to local and global society'

EY Beacon Institute in the *Harvard Business Review*[7]

For the businesses adopting this approach, this necessitates, if there wasn't already, an overt recognition of multiple stakeholder groups that move beyond customers and most often include the world/environment, local communities, employees and, of course, shareholders.

However, a purpose is not the same as a full positioning statement and its impact has been at a more general and higher level, looking at redefining the businesses' role within society. In some cases a brand purpose exists alongside but separate from the brand positioning.

There are still many brand positioning models that are still really glorified brand proposition models and fall into the trap of being oversimplified and too singular in their focus. They fail to distinguish between the need to express a brand's overall and long-lasting philosophy and the range of potentially changing and evolving propositions that a modern-day brand needs. A brand purpose can be seen to be part of an overall brand philosophy, but again it is not a philosophy in its entirety.

Furthermore, as we have discussed, branding has evolved from single products or services with a core target audience and a single-minded proposition to portfolios of products and services with multiple target groups and multiple propositions using multiple media and recognizing multiple touchpoints. It is no longer sensible to think of proposition and positioning as almost interchangeable.

So the difference is...

Returning to the second question from the beginning of this chapter, 'What is the difference between branding and marketing?', hopefully the answer is now clear. Marketing focuses on the way in which the brand goes to market while branding is focused on defining the long-term philosophy of the brand.

From the CIM definition and discussion around proposition development I have argued that marketing's role is to gain insights into what potential customers really want, and what drives and motivates them, so companies are able to develop and market products and services that are relevant and appealing to them and likely to succeed in the long run. It is about defining what should be taken to market and how the brand should go to market.

Drawing a deliberately extreme parallel, branding is more akin to a religion. Branding in its purest sense is about defining the core purpose and philosophy of a brand, its fundamental raison d'être and the principles on which it operates.

Marketing can therefore be seen as working out how best to translate that purpose and philosophy into products and services and how they can best be delivered to the market in ways that will appeal to potential customers. It is from reconciling the needs of the philosophy of the brand with the needs of the customer that brand distinctiveness evolves. If marketing just takes account of what the customer wants it will produce generic products and services and communications; if it just takes account of the brand philosophy it may not present those products and services in ways that appeal to customers.

It is this balancing act that highlights the fact that for many marketers the customer is king, while for brand purists the customer is only one stakeholder and probably not the most important one in defining the brand. And returning to the earlier analogy, this would mean that branding is writing the 'bible' and sales and marketing is writing the 'playbook'.

The different roles of the customer

Marketing should be customer-led.

Customer understanding and insight are fundamental to good marketing and indeed to success in sales, and there is a strong argument that when developing a specific proposition for a brand (or sub-brand or specific product or service) the target audience, the customer, needs to be at the heart of what is being developed. A better understanding of your customer and their motivations can help you develop a better offer, one that is more appealing and engaging for them. One that is tailored to, and for, them. So the current 'positioning' models, are actually more like frameworks for proposition development and are, in fact, eminently suitable for this sort of work even if they are mislabelled.

As I suggested earlier, in practice, owing to the cost of new capital investment and the benefits of using existing infrastructure, some marketing departments' job has become to try to increase the penetration or frequency of usage of existing products and services. In other words, it is to 'sell' more of what they currently offer profitably. Again, this is where a clear understanding of customers' needs and motivations can help, but it is also the point at which the division between marketing and sales starts to blur, as marketing moves closer to the shorter-term sales approach.

Customer understanding needs to be at the heart of proposition development. Good marketing is about understanding customers and their needs, but as discussed branding isn't the same as marketing. The basic tenets are different. For brands and their positioning, the customer isn't necessarily king.

Customer understanding is also one, though not the only, starting point for innovation. Identifying unmet customer needs or how existing needs can be better met are both valuable sources of opportunities. However, ideally, any innovation should then be executed in a way that is distinctive to the brand.

For a brand positioning, a philosophy, you need to start with the brand itself not the customer. You need to start with the business that owns it, you need to take into account the competitive context and all the different stakeholder groups, obviously including various subsets of different customer target groups. It isn't as simple as just giving one particular subset of customers what they want. A modern brand positioning needs to be based on the purpose, the beliefs and its personality, namely the philosophy of the brand.

Working inside out

If every brand owner was to put the customers' desires and needs at the heart of their brand, and to make those consumers their masters then the ultimate result could, and indeed perhaps would, be that all brands in a given market or category would all end up in the same places. In the search for insights to build those brands on, an awful lot of intelligent people working for a lot of large companies would be asking the same sorts of consumers the same sorts of questions, often in the same way and, not surprisingly, they would get to similar sorts of answers.

If this sounds somehow familiar and maybe even frightening, that's because it is something that we are starting to see in a number of different markets, as all those intelligent brand teams and their agencies scramble to find the latest insights in the beer, telecoms, digital games or financial services market and react accordingly.

In these and a number of other markets, there has already been an increasing homogenization of the brand propositions and in new product and service development. If this trend continues to move into brand positioning development it will be a recipe for dullness not distinctiveness. Unless something changes, there will be a further reduction in real brand distinctiveness, which in turn will lead to a reduction in real choice. Consumers will not be able to see any difference between your, and your competitors', brand and will have no basis on which to choose yours – unless, of course, it's cheaper which is not always a recipe for profitability.

As I have argued earlier, 'the vision thing' is an undervalued concept in branding. To have a vision, the belief that what you are doing is right even when those around, let alone customers, do not appear to agree with you can be the difference between another me-too business and a differentiated brand.

In fact, looking at the history of brands, many of the world's most famous brands weren't founded on some startling new customer insight but rather they grew out of 'the vision thing', the beliefs and the drive – the vision of their founders. Others were built on pieces of technology and others even more mundanely were created out of a founder's desire to build a successful business:

- It was the beliefs and values of Anita Roddick that shaped and helped her create The Body Shop.

- Phil Knight created the Nike brand based on what his experience and expertise told him was right for the athletes he coached.

- Microsoft wasn't built on consumer understanding, but on technological development.

- Richard Branson has said that all the insight he needed to create Virgin Atlantic was one phone call or rather the lack of one: 'I decided that there must be room for another airline after I spent two days trying to get through to People's Express, that was the sum of my market research.'[8]

- James Watt of rapidly expanding BrewDog says:

'Businesses fail. Businesses die. Businesses fade into oblivion.

Revolutions never die.

So start a revolution not a business.

It is no longer enough just to start a business. You need a clear purpose, a mission, a reason for existing. Martin [Dickie – his best friend and business partner] and I did not just start a brewery – we set out on a mission to make other people as passionate about great beer as we are. This promise and premise underpins every single thing we do and acts as a resolute reference point for every single decision we make.'[9]

All these brands have benefited from great marketing over the years, but the core of these brands and how they have positioned themselves comes not from their customers, but from the brands themselves, the people and the businesses that founded them and owned them.

In these examples, the brands' (founders') vision and beliefs were king. Customers have undoubtedly helped shape the subsequently launched brands but the customers didn't actually define them. These brands were successful because they answered customer needs but they weren't led by customers overtly. As Steve Jobs said in an interview with *Businessweek* in 1998: 'it's really hard to design products by focus groups. A lot of times, people don't know what they want until you show it to them.'[10]

Most of the brands above and many, many more brands were ones that identified a purpose. A set of beliefs translated those into products and services to which people have been 'converted', whether by great product performance, a strong business model or by great marketing.

Importantly, what these brands do now and what they'll do in the future isn't simply dictated by what the customer wants. What they do and how they do it will be shaped by their brand's philosophy, its fundamental beliefs and principles and, indeed, the needs of the business as well as understanding their customers' needs and motivations.

Finally, I would restate that the customer isn't king when it comes to brand positioning because other stakeholders are equally as important. As I have discussed earlier the best brands come from within. Brands, especially service brands and corporate brands but also many classic FMCG brands, are based on what (who) they are, what they stand for, their people and how those people act.

The best service and corporate brands work from the inside out. They are not just the external face of the organization, but the internal culture and philosophy of the organization. This philosophy will have been shaped not just by past customers but by the history of the organization, the beliefs and values of its founders and leaders, its aims and business strategies and the competitive context it has lived in.

In short, branding isn't just about what you offer (physically) but the way, the style, in which you do it. It's about the brand's culture and service philosophy.

Branding is therefore customer-fed, and not customer-led.

Brand, new thinking

Interestingly, in the last couple of years perhaps the two most important books on marketing and branding have been Byron Sharp's *How Brands Grow* and Jim Stengel's *Grow*, which enter into the debate about the difference between branding and marketing.

Professor Byron Sharp is a highly regarded marketing academic. He has helped turn the Ehrenberg-Bass Institute into one of the most important centres for brand strategy in the world. In *How Brands Grow* he argues against what he calls the Marketing Untruths – fundamental concepts which many in the industry have long held to be the laws of marketing:

- Brand differentiation is a vital marketing task.
- Loyalty metrics reflect brand strength.
- Customer retention is cheaper than acquisition.
- Price promotions boost penetration.
- Who we compete with depends on our brand positioning.

- Mass marketing is dead.
- Buyers have a special reason to buy our brand.
- Our consumers are a distinctive type of person.
- 20 per cent of our customers account for 80 per cent of sales.[11]

Based on his analysis, he suggests a new set of Marketing Laws:

1 Double jeopardy – brands with a smaller market share have far fewer buyers than larger brands, and these fewer buyers are somewhat less loyal.

2 Retention double jeopardy – all brands lose some buyers over time; this loss is proportionate to their market share; big brands lose somewhat less as a proportion of their total customer base.

3 Pareto law – slightly more than 50 per cent of a brand's sales come from 20 per cent of its customers.

4 Attitudes and brand beliefs reflect behavioural loyalty – consumers know more about brands they use than brands they don't use; therefore larger brands score higher on attitude questions because they have more users.

5 Usage drives attitude – buyers of different brands express very similar attitudes and perceptions about their respective brands.

6 Prototypicality – image attributes that describe the product category score higher than less prototypical attributes.

7 Purchase duplication – a brand's customer base overlaps with competitor brands in line with market share.

8 'Buyer moderation' – across two consecutive time periods, some heavy buyers appear to purchase less often, and some light buyers appear to purchase more often; this is largely a statistical artefact.

9 Natural monopoly – bigger brands attract a greater proportion of light category buyers.

10 User bases seldom vary – competing brands sell to very similar customer bases.[12]

His analysis is based on significant amounts of data covering hundreds of product categories and a number of countries provided by, amongst others, The Nielsen Company and TNS.

He recommends brands need to move away from old models of marketing to a new model based on Salience, Distinctiveness, Getting noticed and emotional response, Relevant associations, Building and refreshing memory structures, Reaching and Emotional distracted audiences. It's an approach that has been adopted by a number of the world's leading companies.

Jim Stengel is a highly regarded marketer. He was the global marketing officer at P&G, so held one of the most important branding jobs in the world. Since stepping down from that role, Stengel has become the go-to advocate for brand purpose, which he defines as a 'life-improving ideal' and where that ideal is 'a business's essential reason for being, the higher-order benefit it brings to the world'.

He argues in his book *Grow* that brand purpose, or 'brand ideals', not only represents the right thing to do, but also provide the best route to corporate growth:

> 'Brands build value, whether in consumer products or professional services. Evidence suggests that over a 10-year period, businesses with clearly defined and consistently executed brand purposes deliver on average 400% better returns to shareholders.'[13]

His recommendations are:

- Discover an ideal in one of five fields of fundamental human values (Eliciting joy, Enabling connection, Inspiring exploration, Evoking pride, Positively impacting society).
- Build your culture around your ideal.
- Communicate your ideal to engage employees and customers.
- Deliver a near-ideal customer experience.
- Evaluate your progress and people against your ideal.[14]

One of the questions I have been asked by senior marketing people is whether both approaches can coexist and if so how. For me, rather than being contradictory, I can see how the two books can be seen as complementary and in fact align with the differences between branding and marketing.

Stengelism is rooted in creating a vision or purpose for the brand, which as I have suggested is a key part of defining the brand's long-term philosophy. Stengel is a brand-man and his book to a great extent is about branding.

How Brands Grow is undoubtedly a book that has had a significant impact on marketing thinking and how many marketing departments operate. I would, however, suggest that it is predominantly a marketing book, not a brand book. The title may include the word 'brand' but actually, the meaning of the full title is very much in line with my definition of marketing. The book is focused on how you go to market most effectively, and not on how you define your brand, its positioning and philosophy. The Sharpian mantra is about how to maximize your marketing efficiency. Sharp is a marketing man.

My recommendation to senior marketing managers is to read and learn from both.

In conclusion

I have suggested that, in most markets, sales can be seen as relatively short term (the selling of major capital projects or investments being an obvious exception) and tends to be focused on knowing or understanding the needs and drivers of a single or a few customers or consumers.

Marketing takes, or perhaps more accurately tries to take, a longer-term view. It is focused on generally larger groups of consumers and/or customers and understanding their needs and drives, so it can help organizations satisfy them profitably. However, in the modern world it is under constant and extreme pressure to demonstrate relatively short-term results and is being driven to act in ways that are closer to sales.

Branding is the 'discipline' that takes the longest-term view. The brand is what remains while sales directors, marketing managers, advertising campaigns and promotional offers come and go. Brands can have highs and lows, peaks and troughs.

Branding with one of its roles being to create and manage meaning in customers' minds is long term. It takes both time to build that meaning and time for the consistency of the brand's values to be understood. A brand needs time to demonstrate its consistency in acting in accordance with its values so that consumers can not only recognize them but believe that they are the heart of that brand. If a brand doesn't have any core beliefs or constantly appears to change them, then the understanding and trust that is essential for any brand will be undermined or even destroyed.

In its purest form as a philosophy it is also the least consumer or customer focused. It's not that consumers and customers aren't crucial for a brand's success but rather that a brand has to come from within, to be based on beliefs and principles. This is what differentiates one brand from another.

Notes

1 Popik, B (2017) [accessed 16 January 2017] The Big Apple: 'Half the money spent on advertising is wasted, but no one knows which half' *Barrypopik.com* [Online] http://www.barrypopik.com/index.php/new_york_city/entry/half_the_money_spent_on_advertising_is_wasted_but_no_one_knows_which_half

2 Tesseras, L (2017) [accessed 9 March 2017] Sir Martin Sorrell: Short-termism is the biggest threat to marketers, *Marketing Week* [Online] https://www.marketingweek.com/2017/03/02/sir-martin-sorrell/?cmpid=em~newsletter~breaking_news~n~n&utm_medium=em&utm_source=newsletter&utm_campaign=breaking_news&itx%5bemail%5d=giles.lury@thevalueengineers.com&eid=3156704

3 Ries, A and Trout, J (2001) *Positioning: The Battle for Your Mind*, McGraw-Hill Education, London

4 Lury, A (1994) *Marketing at a Point of Change*, 1st edn, Howell Henry Chaldecott Lury & Partners, London

5 Wnek, M (2000) [accessed 12 January 2017] Agency of the Decade: HHCL & Partners – HHCL proved its mettle with a canny combination of business initiatives and daring creative work such as Tango, setting the pace for advertising in the 90s, *Campaign* [Online] http://www.campaignlive.co.uk/article/agency-decade-hhcl-partners-hhcl-proved-its-mettle-canny-combination-business-initiatives-daring-creative-work-tango-setting-pace-advertising-90s/35096

6 Smith, S and Milligan, A (2015) *On Purpose*, Kogan Page, London

7 EY Beacon Institute (2017) [accessed 12 January 2017] The Business Case for Purpose, *Harvard Business Review* [Online] http://www.ey.com/Publication/vwLUAssets/ey-the-business-case-for-purpose/$FILE/ey-the-business-case-for-purpose.pdf

8 Sampson, A (1996) *Company Man*, 1st edn, HarperCollins, London

9 Watt, J (2015) *Business for Punks*, 1st edn, Portfolio, Penguin, London

10 Steve Jobs on Apple's resurgence (25 May 1998) [accessed 12 January 2017] *Businessweek* [Online] http://www.businessweek.com/bwdaily/dnflash/may1998/nf80512d.htm (subscribers only) or quoted in Chunka Mui [accessed 31 May 2017] Five Dangerous Lessons to Learn From Steve Jobs, *Forbes* [Online] https://www.forbes.com/sites/chunkamui/2011/10/17/five-dangerous-lessons-to-learn-from-steve-jobs/#1754a7a93a95

11 Sharp, B (2010) *How Brands Grow*, 1st edn, Oxford University Press, Oxford

12 Sharp, B (2010) *How Brands Grow*, 1st edn, Oxford University Press, Oxford

13 Stengel, J (2012) *Grow*, 1st edn, Virgin, London

14 Stengel, J (2012) *Grow*, 1st edn, Virgin, London

The need to manage multiplicity

05

'*The singular multiplicity of this universe draws my deepest attention. It is a thing of ultimate beauty.*'
LETO II ATREIDES IN *GOD EMPEROR OF DUNE* BY FRANK HERBERT

Weaving it all together

In keeping with the concept of managing multiplicity, this chapter will aim to weave together the multiple threads that have been developed in the preceding chapters to create a tapestry that makes a compelling case for the need for marketers to manage multiplicity.

Not surprisingly, it will suggest that there is no single reason why marketers need to adopt a broader and more flexible concept of branding; rather it will argue that there are a number of 'threads' each with a number of different 'strands' that make the change a necessity.

The chapter will end by providing a definition and description of what multiplicity in branding means. To do so it will draw on elements from the definitions of multiplicity from psychology and philosophy and the themes discussed.

Multiples of multiples

The reasons why marketers need to more openly embrace complexity and manage multiplicity of brands are rooted in the fact that the roles and social relationships of those brands are no longer singular, they are multifaceted. In fact, these relationships are often multiples of multiples – multiple products and services with multiple stakeholder groups. Brands are striving to engage more often with more groups of people about more products, services and aspects of their brands than ever before. Singular, one size fits all, propositions may have worked well in a simpler world but in a world of multiplicity, they are an idea that is simply out of date. The continued, sometimes subconscious, addiction to the old models and old ideas is dragging brand management down.

The branding thread

Brands are no longer single products (or services) targeted at single target audiences. The concept of branding can be seen as one of the most successful phenomena of the 20th and now the 21st century. It has grown and spread in a variety of ways.

Branding is now applied across multiple categories and classes of brands from services to business-to-business to corporate to destination to not-for-profit to political to famous person to personal brands. The list has grown steadily.

Furthermore, during the last 30 years and in some cases before that, brands have consistently disproved 'the trap of line extension', successfully extending their reach and with that broadening their meaning and the market 'spaces' they compete in. Brands are now portfolios of products and services, not all of which have the same target audience. Brands cross borders and market sectors with equal regularity (if not always ease). A single proposition rarely works well across a whole portfolio of products and services. This is compounded by marketers' lack of clarity about the difference between a specific product's or service's go-to-market proposition and the broader overarching brand positioning, making their jobs even harder in today's more complicated environment.

The notion of branding has also expanded. It now covers not just the original public face of a product – its name, identity and advertising – it now incorporates its values and beliefs, its culture, the experiences and brand encounters it delivers. Brands now have a series of touchpoints or encounters with stakeholders across what they hope is a lifetime relationship. Each encounter is an opportunity to build or damage that relationship. Branding is both an internal and external concept and as such has multiple stakeholders from customers, to key opinion formers, to governments to employees, both current and future potentials. This means that not only does a brand need different propositions and messages for different customer groups; it also needs to manage its relationships and dialogues with these other stakeholders.

The usage of the terms 'branding' and 'marketing' have also become dangerously intertwined and are often used interchangeably so blurring the key distinction between the long-term definition of the DNA of a brand and the shorter term and more changing marketing of that brand. The reality is, in fact, that if anything marketing and sales are getting drawn closer together.

New thinking and new models are therefore required to help marketers manage this complexity. Managing this complexity may be more difficult but who said marketing was meant to be easy?

Indeed, at the Fire Circus conference, 'The Future of Branded Content', and echoing Avis' famous slogan, Emma Jenkins, then Chief Marketing Officer at telecoms brand giffgaff called for marketers to 'try harder': 'If we're asking our customers to engage more with us, shouldn't we be willing to work harder to engage with them?'[1]

Brands are built on relationships and relationships are rarely simple or uni-dimensional. In fact, this is the reason that marketing is so interesting, so challenging, and so much fun for so many of its participants.

The media thread

The ongoing metamorphosis of media cannot be overemphasized. The unprecedented growth in the scale and variety of media has transformed the way we live and the way most industries operate. Branding and marketing are just two other industries where those changes have been fundamental. From an era where there were limited opportunities for brands to make what were predominately one-way sales pitches, we now live in an age where there are endless means of engaging in real-time multi-participant brand-related discussions and dialogues with people right around the world... or even in space.

On 21 July 1969, just after 02.30 (UTC), Neil Armstrong opened the hatch and began his descent. On stepping onto the surface of the moon, he spoke the now historic words: 'That's one small step for [a] man, one giant leap for mankind'. It was broadcast by all three UK channels (BBC1, BBC2 and ITV) and seen mostly in black and white (colour TV had been launched in the UK only in July 1967).[2]

The Command Module *Columbia* returned to Earth on 24 July and the astronauts began 21 days of quarantine. So it wasn't until 13 August that there was a parade in their honour in New York. As they entered Times Square, the three astronauts were greeted by a flashing sign which read 'Welcome home to planet Earth, home of Coca-Cola'.[3]

Fast-forward to 2015–16 and Tim Peake, the British astronaut, completes a 186-day Principia mission working on the International Space Station. While in space, he regularly chatted live to different media outlets and stations, answered e-mails not only from his family but also from schools, other educational institutions and the general public. In February 2016, he appeared 'live' from space at the Brit Awards where he reduced the pop star Adele to tears when presenting her with a Global Success award. During his voyage, he had 1,672,203 social media followers on Twitter, Facebook, Flickr and Instagram. On 24 December 2015 he tweeted: 'I'd like to apologise to the lady I just called by mistake saying "Hello, is this planet Earth?" – not a prank call... just a wrong number!'[4]

Media has come or rather gone a long way in less than 50 years. The content of that media has also changed enormously, not just the amount of content that is now generated every day but the tone and style of that content and the speed at which it can be shared. As one colleague recently said to me: 'Knowledge is no longer power, it's available to everyone at the click of a keyboard button'.

At random, I put the word 'Bullfrog' into Google and 801,000 results came up in 0.65 seconds. When I put in the word 'brands' there were 1,210,000,000 results in 0.76 seconds. Knowledge on these subjects is now just a click away.

However, it's not just the number of channels that has changed; the tone of most communications has evolved. It has become a lot less formal. There are the new languages of 'texting' or 'emoji', and new acronyms abound. Language and imagery has changed reflecting social changes too. The roles of race and gender are now often depicted very differently. These changes have been reflected in brand communications too, though it has taken its time to change and may still need to change more.

Despite David Ogilvy's famous (and un-PC) advice… 'the consumer isn't a moron she's your wife'[5] … a considerable amount of brand communication from the latter half of the 20th century was not only sexist, but condescending as well, talking down to the 'little housewife'. There are still exceptions but brand conversations have become more adult-to-adult and recently major advertisers have promised to clean up their acts even more. *Campaign* magazine reported in June 2016 that: 'Unilever has pledged to stamp out female stereotypes in its ads, after finding more progressive campaigns play better with their target audience.'[6]

Speaking at Cannes Lions 2016, chief marketing officer Keith Weed unveiled internal Unilever research analysing 1,000 ads from different countries and found 50 per cent contained stereotypical portrayals of women. Just 1 per cent conveyed women as funny, 2 per cent showed them as intelligent, and 3 per cent showed them as leaders.[7]

The research examined Unilever's own advertising output, split into 'progressive' and 'normative', and found that the more progressive ads resonated better with audiences.[8] According to Weed, the ads had 12 per cent greater impact, in terms of consumers actively enjoying and feeling involved with the ads.[9]

Weed went on to say:

'This is not a moral issue, it's an economic issue. We will create better advertising if we create advertising that is more progressive and start challenging those stereotypes.'[10]

Another fundamental change is that the role of much marketing communication has shifted from interruption to engagement. Rather than interrupting your favourite TV programme they want to provide content that will be interesting enough and with which you want to engage. This has led to a corresponding increase in the amount of content that brands and indeed their followers generate.

This explosion in the volume of branded content across the huge variety of media means that just repeating the same single-minded message is going to be not only repetitive but downright boring and/ or annoying. Brands need more breadth to their messaging if they want to remain interesting and engaging. They can no longer afford to oversimplify.

This diversity has also led to a fragmentation of control even within brand owners. As Paul Gaskell pointed out in in his paper 'Manage Complexity, Win Awards':

> 'Central brand functions have been joined by new teams that have been created as fast as each new digital channel emerges, and each new team redefines the brand in its own way: In a way that fits the channel.'[11]

As he goes on to explain, this is another challenge to the old model and highlights the need for new and different ones:

> 'Consequently, the now rather old-fashioned brand positioning state-ments on which the branding industry has focused for so long have often ended up confined to a desk drawer to gather dust. The structure and strategy that these documents provided has been cast aside.'[12]

While this further makes the case for managing multiplicity it doesn't mean there is no role for some element of simplification. This demand for some simplification remains apparent: for example, in the 140-character limit on Twitter and the 60-second maximum on Instagram.

The customer thread

It is clear that the world has changed enormously in the last 30 years and at a rate that is faster than we have ever seen before. What's more it is still changing and the rate of that change may well be accelerat-ing. Cataloguing all the changes would be a subject for another whole book but it is clear that some of the changes are influencing people's relationship with brands and the complexity of those relationships.

People in discussion groups will nowadays talk knowledgeably about BOGOFs (Buy one get one free offers) and eloquently about the use of sans serif fonts. People are now not just media-literate, they are marketing-literate too. They have been there, seen that and bought the T-shirt.

People know about marketing, they know more about brands and branding than they have ever done. They recognize classic marketing approaches and while many may still go for them, others are actively rebelling. Consequently, brands need to find new ways with which to engage and stay engaged with these more sophisticated customers.

In fact, the relationship between brands and customers could be described as a love–hate one. There are more people who love certain brands and there are more people who hate the notion of marketing. Relationships with brands have become more extreme as brand and the role of marketing have become more open.

Some people will join Facebook groups of their favourite brands. Some will be brand advocates championing brands to friends and family. Others will become unpaid walking billboards for them, sporting their logos and tagline across their chests with branded T-shirts and sweatshirts.

Equally, there are others who are aggressively anti-brand and rather than thinking of a brand as a promise they will think brands are just unfulfilled promises. Promises, promises, anything to get your money. Naomi Klein's book *No Logo: Taking aim at the brand bullies* is just one of the anti-brand manifestos. Various brand scandals and disasters, like the recent VW Dieselgate scandal further undermine people's trust in specific brands and for some brands in general.[13]

There will be many others, probably the majority, sitting somewhere on a spectrum between these two extremes.

It is probably fair to say that in general more people want more of brands. There is a realism whereby people recognize that brands need to be profitable but on the other hand they want them to contribute more to society and to be more conscious of the world's limited resources and use them more carefully.

There are many surveys that show people increasingly want, and feel more affinity to, brands that serve a higher purpose. People say they want brands that do more than make a profit, but also operate responsibly to address social and environmental issues. One example is an international study by Unilever that revealed that a third of consumers (33 per cent) are now choosing to buy from brands they believe are doing social or environmental good.[14]

For many brands, this is another layer of complexity that they are or need to consider and suggests another layer or element of multiplicity they must address. In Chapter 1, I highlighted that in a world that many people think is now more complex, more chaotic than ever before, there is a huge appeal in the apparent speed and ease of simplicity. There is an interesting paradox of choice: people have long asked for more personalization and more options, but when confronted with the reality and sheer scale of the sort of choice that is now available they find it increasingly difficult to make a decision. It's a world that for many feels cash richer but time poorer, so there is a desire for soundbites, KISS-ing and the notion of simplicity.

However, this is only part of the story; not everything is being made shorter or more simplistic or single-minded. Take television, a natural home of the soundbite society you might think, but in reality it is not all short, single-minded snippets.

What are some of the biggest trends in television and television programmes? Well, in addition to streaming of content, which is redefining the way people see programme schedules, there are other trends, which suggest there is something to be found in richness and depth. Firstly, there is the emergence of binge watching, whereby people watch two, four, six or eight hours in one sitting, whether streamed or as part of a box set. The appeal appears to be the opportunity to get truly immersed in and 'binge' on the storylines and the characters. Secondly and perhaps in some way linked to binge watching, there has been significant growth in the number of major series, each of which comprises several seasons each with 20+ episodes. There is huge appeal and global impact of series like *24*, *Game of Thrones*, *House of Cards*, *Lost*, *Westworld* and *Madmen*, whether they are watched weekly or binged upon.

These series are often complex, multi-layered and have multiple storylines. They have the time to develop characters, plots and subplots. In fact, their mantra seems to be 'keep it complex, stupid'.

Customers, people have adapted to change and their relationship and expectations of brands and their communication has changed too. While it would be easy to say that the world is even more over-communicated so the need for oversimplified communication is even greater, it would be completely the wrong thing to do.

The tapestry

Weaving this together there are at least three broad threads – branding, media and customers – each made up of a number of strands.

Branding

- Branding is now applied to many more categories than just fast-moving consumer goods.
- Each brand is generally a portfolio of different products and services.
- Branding offers different specific benefits to different specific audiences and is expected to engage internal audiences as well.

Media

- The media world has exploded and there are thousands more channels.
- Digital and social media mean that people can now converse with each other much more easily and regularly, and similarly can engage with, or about, brands much more easily and frequently.
- Brands are no longer the only content creators; user-created content far exceeds many brands' output.
- Marketing communication is shifting from the old interruption model to a new engagement one.

Customers

- People – customers – are no longer just media-literate, they are marketing-literate too. They know and expect more of brands.

- While more people still claim to be influenced by a brand's purpose and values than actually act on them, it does appear that this is a trend that is growing.

- People are also wonderfully contrary, as humans so often are; they are drawn both to simplification and short forms but at the same time also want the interest, enjoyment and depth of a longer form of engagement too.

The old models of singularity and old reductionist thinking are out of date and do not reflect or embrace the new reality. Being single-minded is, in fact, being narrow-minded. The drive for oversimplification should be over. Marketers need to embrace and manage multiplicity.

Towards a definition of multiplicity

If this is true then there is a case for embracing this increased complexity and managing multiplicity, but what exactly do we mean by multiplicity? Nowadays and in mainstream usage, 'multiplicity' means either a large number, or a state of being that is various or manifold.

However, the term 'multiplicity' was initially used to describe a phenomenon in mathematics, where the multiplicity of a member of a multiset is the number of times it appears in the multiset. For example, the number of times a given polynomial equation has a root at a given point. This notion of multiplicity is important to be able to count correctly without specifying exceptions (for example, double roots counted twice). Hence the expression, 'counted with multiplicity'.

The multiplicity term, however, has been adopted by other disciplines where it has been given specific and probably easier to understand definitions relevant to those subjects. It is some of these that are more useful in suggesting how the term might be applied to branding.

The French philosopher Gilles Deleuze (1925–95) adopted multiplicity as a philosophical term. He used the term to describe thought phenomena that are in constant flux. He defined multiplicity as:

'an entity that originates from a folding or twisting of simple elements. Like a sand dune, a multiplicity is in constant flux, though it attains some consistency for a short or long duration. A multiplicity has porous boundaries and is defined provisionally by its variation and dimensions.'[15]

As mentioned earlier (in Chapter 1), in psychology 'multiplicity' has been defined as the everyday use of multiple personality styles by a single person; how a person adopts and adapts their personality style depending on the situation they are in, whom they are with and what role they are playing.

These two definitions provide an interesting basis for defining multiplicity in branding; they capture elements that are true of all modern brands and which are not often reflected in many of the current definitions and explanations of branding.

Firstly, Deleuze's definition captures the powerful notion of something that is constantly changing – and evolving, that has 'porous boundaries', but is still a coherent entity, in his case the analogy of the sand dune. A modern brand is like an organic entity constantly growing and changing; new products and services are added, pricing and distribution change, new communications are developed and shared, new customers buy into the brand, others may be tempted away, the workforce changes. Sometimes even the brand name and/or its identity changes yet the brand 'entity' remains. A brand is not a static or consistent concept but it is one that 'attains some consistency for a short or [hopefully a] long duration'.

Secondly the notion of a single brand having multiple personalities is one that appears to contradict much traditional marketing theory and yet when considered in the context of what a modern brand is expected to do it seems remarkably sensible. As discussed, brands have many different stakeholders and play different roles for them, so coherency rather than outright consistency has to be a more practical approach. Adapting what you say and do and where you say it is key to ensuring you get the engagement you want.

Today's brands need to be flexible and adaptable. They need a broad functional and emotional repertoire. They need to be able to engage different audiences through different media but those messages and encounters need to relate and be shaped by an overall brand philosophy – its editorial standpoint. Brands that can do this are complex, not chaotic. They are multidimensional. Brands manging this multiplicity can talk about different things to different people in different ways, and not be seen as schizophrenic. They are not so much consistent as coherent.

It is not a complete shift from the strategic and regimented monoliths of the old approach to a complete and chaotic tactical free-for-all. It's not a regimental square but neither is it the Mongol hordes. It is a move away from 'all singing off the same song sheet' towards a more orchestral approach. The best modern brands are like symphonies with the richness, depth and variety to create greater emotional resonance and attachment.

Much of this book has been talking around the notion of multiplicity and brand multiplicity in particular; however, no formal definition has yet been put forward until now. Brand multiplicity is a term used to express the true complexity and constantly evolving multifaceted nature of brands and their relationships with multiple groups of different stakeholders.

The definition aims to reflect that most brands:

- are no longer a single product or service but cover a regularly evolving range of products and services, both directly under the master brand or as sub-brands;
- often cross not only countries, but also markets and categories;
- have a wide range of different stakeholder groups, both internal and external, who have different needs and priorities and respond differently to different messages and media;
- are not static entities, but are in a constant state of change. Major elements can and do change but the central concept of the brand, its purpose and its philosophy remain consistent for longer periods of time.

It runs counter to much of current branding theory and practice, which has been reductionist, and instead embraces, even champions, complexity.

In conclusion

Managing multiplicity is therefore akin to being a musical conductor. Conductors need to know the overall score and the end result they want to achieve. To do this they bring in different parts of the orchestra as and when they are required and guide and shape their performance.

A brand conductor has the complicated and challenging task of simultaneously maximizing the performance of their brand across a range of different stakeholder groups. It is about having the ability to truly understand what lies at the heart of your brand – its purpose, its core beliefs – and help find the ways with which to bring these to the different stakeholder groups gaining the greatest and most valuable engagement.

It's about conducting a beautiful symphony, not allowing a chaotic cacophony or trying to reduce your brand to a mundane monotone.

It's time for a new model, a new framework, one that helps marketers manage multiplicity that encompasses all that a brand is and allows them the necessary greater executional flexibility while still maintaining a long-term strategic brand focus.

Notes

1 Jenkins, E (2013) [accessed 13 January 2017] In: *The Future of Branded Content* [Online] http://www.firecircus.co.uk/the-future-of-branded-content-presentations/

2 NASA (2014) [accessed 13 January 2017] July 20, 1969: One Giant Leap For Mankind [Online] https://www.nasa.gov/mission_pages/apollo/apollo11.html

3 *The Guardian* (2001) [accessed 13 January 2017] A brief history of brands: Coca-Cola [Online] https://www.theguardian.com/media/2001/jul/09/marketingandpr.g21

4 Peake, T (2015) [accessed 13 January 2017] I'd like to apologise to the lady I just called by mistake saying "Hello, is this planet Earth?" – not a prank call... just a wrong number! *Twitter* 24/12 [Online] www.twitter.com

5 Ogilvy, D (1964) *Confessions of an Advertising Man*, 1st edn, p 96, Ballantine Books, New York

6 Ghosh, S (2016) [accessed 13 January 2017] No more 'vacuous' women in ads, says Unilever's Keith Weed, *Campaign* [Online] http://www.campaignlive.co.uk/article/no-vacuous-women-ads-says-unilevers-keith-weed/1399998

7 Weed, K (2016) [accessed 13 January 2017] In: The Future of Brands [Online] http://www.jwt.com/blog/cannes-lions-2016/cannes-lions-2016-the-future-of-brands-with-unilevers-keith-weed/

8 Weed, K (2016) [accessed 13 January 2017] In: The Future of Brands [Online] http://www.jwt.com/blog/cannes-lions-2016/cannes-lions-2016-the-future-of-brands-with-unilevers-keith-weed/

9 Weed, K (2016) [accessed 13 January 2017] In: The Future of Brands [Online] http://www.jwt.com/blog/cannes-lions-2016/cannes-lions-2016-the-future-of-brands-with-unilevers-keith-weed/

10 Weed, K (2016) [accessed 13 January 2017] In: The Future of Brands [Online] http://www.jwt.com/blog/cannes-lions-2016/cannes-lions-2016-the-future-of-brands-with-unilevers-keith-weed/

11 Managing Multiplicity (2013) In: The Value Engineering 2013 conference, Tokyo, The Institute of Value Management

12 Managing Multiplicity (2013) In: The Value Engineering 2013 conference, Tokyo, The Institute of Value Management

13 Klein, N (2000) *No Logo: Taking aim at the brand bullies*, 1st edn, Flamingo, London

14 Unilever (2017) [accessed 9 March 2017] Report shows a third of consumers prefer sustainable brands [Online] https://www.unilever.com/news/press-releases/2017/report-shows-a-third-of-consumers-prefer-sustainable-brands.html

15 Deleuze, G (2008) Gilles Deleuze, In: *Stanford Encyclopaedia of Philosophy*, 1st edn, Stanford

A framework for managing multiplicity

06

'Variety is the very spice of life, that gives it all its flavour.'
WILLIAM COWPER FROM HIS POEM 'THE TASK' (1785)

Unfit for purpose

Most of the current brand positioning models are unfit for their stated purpose.

Most of them, like the brand pyramid shown in Figure 6.1,[1] are designed to fit on a single page and are depicted as a single shape. As a

Figure 6.1 A brand pyramid, a classic brand model

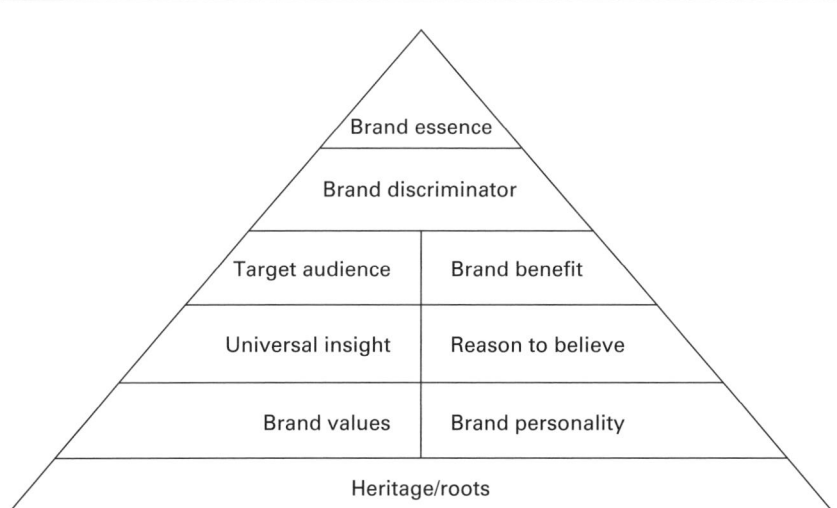

SOURCE Cool Avenues (see Note 1) adapted by the author

result, the brand teams who complete them are encouraged to reduce, merge and simplify things. This can lead to oversimplification.

Part of the simplification inherent in many of the current models is that they are based on understanding the needs and motivations of a specific target group and so identifying a single proposition, which works for that segment. The weakness with this is that, as we have seen, brands must now address multiple and differentiated target groups at the same time.

The increasing pressure for marketers to deliver short-term results further means teams focus on propositions – what will drive sales in the short run. The focus is on the brand discriminator and the brand benefit (the proposition). This makes them less like an overall brand positioning model and more akin to a brand proposition framework.

The current models therefore simply aren't very good as models for brand definition and positioning. They are used too often to develop targeted brand propositions. This doesn't mean, however, that the thinking they represent isn't useful. It is. If viewed as a brand proposition model, rather than a brand positioning model, then they are still very relevant and useful for marketing departments today.

However, in the new brandscape marketers need to learn to accept and manage brand multiplicity. They have to accept, no embrace, that any brand can and should have more than one proposition at any point in time. One brand can and should have a number of different propositions all co-existing successfully at the same time. They need to develop a range of effective propositions for the many products and services provided under any one brand.

Another reason why the current models and brand positioning models may not align is that, as I have suggested, marketing and branding are very different animals. While developing a specific proposition, the consumer may be 'king'; in the creation of a brand and in defining its raison d'être the consumer is only one possible source of inspiration. The other sources, which in many, maybe most, cases are much more important, are the brand's owners and founders.

There are a number of other specific weaknesses of the current models, which will be discussed in later chapters. For example, many of the current models have sections for both values and personality and, in practice, brand values and the brand's personality are often confused and indeed sometimes clumped together. Furthermore, too often brands use the same bland but positive 'apple-pie and motherhood' type expressions as values. I believe that brand values are better expressed as brand beliefs or principles and that when defined as such can then be crucial to the definition of a brand and its positioning (see Chapter 7).

A new framework is required

What is required is a new model; or rather, a new framework as this suggests a larger description of the underlying structure of a whole system. A model tends to be a 'graphical, mathematical (symbolic), physical, or verbal representation or simplified version of a concept'.[2]

The Marketing Complex Framework I am suggesting (Figure 6.2) and with which we have worked with a number of clients allows for a separation between the more long-term and consistent core of a brand, the brand's philosophy and a number of shorter term, more changeable, specific propositions that all sit under that one brand name (and sub-brands if they exist).

Figure 6.2   The new Marketing Complex Framework

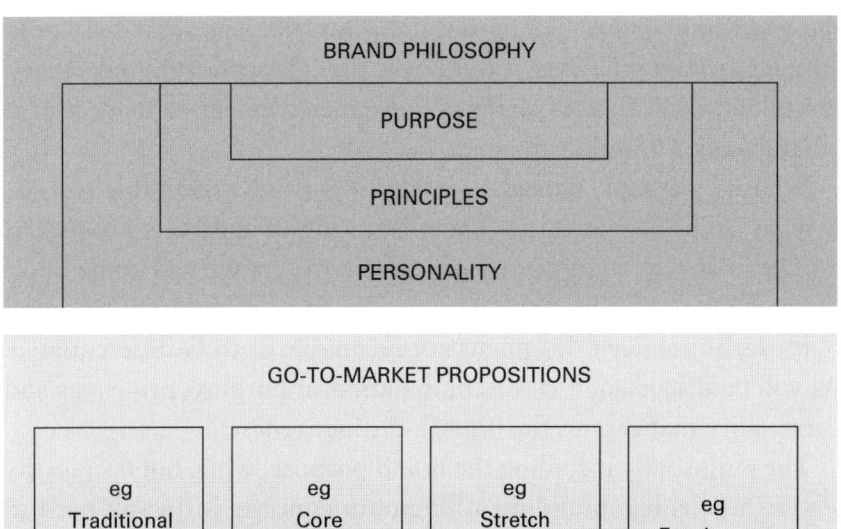

It is a multipart framework. As such, it may lose that soundbite, all-on-one-page desirability that our reductionist society so likes, but what it gains is flexibility and depth.

This separation of the two elements is crucial as it is this flexibility that allows this new multipart framework to handle the complexities, the depth and the varieties of target groups, the different propositions that a modern brand must have to succeed. It reflects the difference between branding and marketing.

The long-term brand philosophy

The first section of the new multipart framework is the core brand philosophy. This is the branding part of the framework. Rather than working to distil the brand to an essence and/or focus on the proposition, it is a description of the purpose, the principles and the personality of the brand. It is the 'why' and 'who' of the brand. It should describe its long-term vision, its approach to what it does; the system of principles that guides it in practice, and the style it adopts.

It is the part that is focused on the long-term central unchanging purpose and core of the brand. This is the DNA of the brand, the heart and soul of the brand, the principle. It is what the brand remains true to whatever it does over time. It serves to guide brand behaviour, regardless of channel, consumer segment or market. It is what makes a brand distinctive.

What is, perhaps, almost as interesting as what is in this section, is what isn't in this section. There is no target audience, no insight, no frame of reference, no reasons to believe. As we will come on to see, there may well be some form of benefit or promise in the brand purpose, but in itself this might not be unique or truly differentiated. As will be discussed, it is the combination of purpose, principles and personality that creates the brand's distinctiveness.

The philosophy including the brand purpose, while not necessarily set in stone is like branding a long-term concept. It doesn't need to change every time the advertising campaign does.

Take, for example, what was, on the face of it, a dramatic shift in BMW's advertising, where it moved away from its long-term strapline of 'The Ultimate Driving Machine' to the clearly more emotive 'Joy'.

The Wall Street Journal reported on 14 February 2010 (an auspicious date for a shift to a more emotion-led line) that Jack Pitney, Vice President of Marketing at BMW for North America said: 'The new 'Joy' campaign is a big departure for us… We hope to really add some humanity to our brand.'[3]

For many, this appeared to be a change in the brand's purpose; a change from an engineering-led benefit to an emotionally-led benefit. While it was indeed a radical shift in the brand's marketing, it wasn't actually a change to the brand's long-term purpose and philosophy. It was a change in how the brand went to market and not a fundamental change to the brand itself.

'Joy' was a new advertising expression of the brand's proposition. Its long-term purpose remained the same; a commitment to use its engineering expertise to drive great driving experiences – sheer driving pleasure. The new copy on the corporate website in 2012 reiterated the commitment to driving pleasure, but reflected the greater emphasis on the emotional side of that purpose – the pleasure, the joy. What Jack Pitney and his marketing team felt was the best way to market the brand at that time.

'We are BMW. We don't just build cars, we create emotions – enthusiasm, fascination, goose bumps guaranteed.

Sheer driving pleasure is our top priority. And so that it never ends, we constantly reinvent it. Making it more intelligent, more efficient, more dynamic. Because joy is what drives us – this most personal of feelings, in all its many different forms: Besides sheer driving pleasure, what matters to us is the joy of owning something very special, the joy of real values such as responsibility and recognition; the joy of success and progress. And not least, the pure joy of living. Joy is BMW.'[4]

Four years on, the latest ads don't sign off with 'Joy' but still use 'The ultimate driving machine' line and the website reads a bit differently too:

> 'The BMW brand epitomises Sheer Driving Pleasure – past, present and into the next 100 years. BMW aims to make this fascinating driving experience even more intense in the future. The driver is in constant communication with the vehicle in an intuitive and natural way. At the same time, the vehicle expands the driver's range of perception and transforms him or her into the 'Ultimate Driver' – the best driver they can possibly be. The Companion responds to the driver's personal needs in order to create emotionally-intense experiences.'[5]

In this copy, there is no explicit mention of joy, but still there right at the beginning is that long-term commitment to 'Sheer driving pleasure'.

The core philosophy of a brand doesn't need to be redefined every time a new product is launched, a new target is engaged or a new advertising tagline created.

A brand's DNA and the missing 5 per cent

The initial analogy with DNA is a deliberate and, I believe, very good one. Everyone has a unique and distinctive DNA; it is our individual biological marker.

While everybody is an individual, over 95 per cent of all humans' DNAs are identical. It is only 5 per cent that distinguishes us from everybody else. We have lots of similarities but a small part that differentiates us. We are all human beings. We all breathe air and need food and water to keep us alive. Yet despite many similarities we are still all individuals.

The parallel with brands is strong. In the same way that we are all individuals, every brand is individual... yet the majority of their stated DNAs are similar.

Identifying and categorizing what really makes a brand distinctive is a skill. It is a skill that isn't helped by the use of values in many brand models as, in practice, the ones selected by marketers tend to be the bland, generic ones. The focus is on similarities not on differences.

This parallel, along with a more detailed description and suggestions for developing purpose, principles and personality will be discussed further in the following chapters.

The go-to-market propositions

The second section of the new multipart framework contains the multiple go-to-market propositions. These are evolving expressions of the brand's products and services, its communications and touchpoints that are adapted to different target groups, products, channels or markets. It is the marketing-focused part of the framework.

Each proposition should include 'Who are we targeting?' (the target group) and what insights do we have into what drives their motivations and behaviours, 'What's in it for them?' (benefits) and lastly, 'Why should they believe us?' (reasons-to-believe). All of which are included in most brand models nowadays but only once.

Propositions are shorter term and more focused on a current offer. They should be both tactically flexible and strategically robust. As such, they provide the flexibility required to deliver the depth and range of propositions and content required for a modern brand and its ever-changing nature, while the core elements of the philosophy ensure that they do so in a way that is in alignment with the brand strategy. They should be coherent not blindly and blandly consistent. Separate propositions can be developed for different products and services and/ or for different specific targets for a specific product or service.

The propositions can and, in fact, should evolve as the market, customer tastes and expectations change. New propositions can be added to as new products and services are launched.

It is this flexibility that is one of the most important differences between this framework and most other models. Rather than just the single brand proposition contained in most current models, this new framework is designed to incorporate a number of different propositions simultaneously.

The propositions allow for a more nuanced approach to different target groups, whether they are customers, investors, employees or the local community. Rather than trying to apply a one-size-fits-all approach, the model assumes that different segments – or even the same segment using different channels – will require subtly or sometimes significantly different propositions, all built out from a single brand philosophy.

One writer who has argued for this to a certain extent is Geoffrey Moore who, in his book *Crossing the Chasm*, puts the case for fundamentally different marketing approaches for technology brands when targeting early adopters and mainstream users. It is this element of the framework that reflects the growth of different target groups and the likely further expansion of the number of channels and the number of consumer segments and other target groups that brands will need to engage with.

In developing these propositions, and in line with this section being marketing focused it is a deep understanding of the different groups, including consumers, that enables brands to reach out and engage these audiences effectively. Understanding the needs and motivations of these groups will be key to developing powerful propositions.

To successfully engage a variety of segments across multiple channels and markets, marketers need a deeper understanding of these groups than that on which they have historically relied. Marketers need to understand how they perceive their brand and how they wish to engage across each channel and at each point in their journey with that brand.

Without this, all the hard work of defining the brand could be for nothing. The brand's philosophy needs to be translated into propositions that will connect and motivate their target audiences.

A real-world example

Including real-world examples in books like these is always desirable but many clients quite rightly would like to maintain confidentiality.

The full framework that follows may not be exactly how Sir Richard Branson would define the Virgin brand but anyone who has heard him speak about Virgin or has read his book, *The Virgin Way: How to listen, learn, laugh and lead*, should recognize what I have put together. Sir Richard Branson and his numerous teams are some of the leading lights of marketers who have embraced multiplicity, so I make no excuses for using them as an example again to show how the full model might work (Figure 6.3).

Figure 6.3 Example of how Virgin could be expressed in the new Marketing Complex Framework

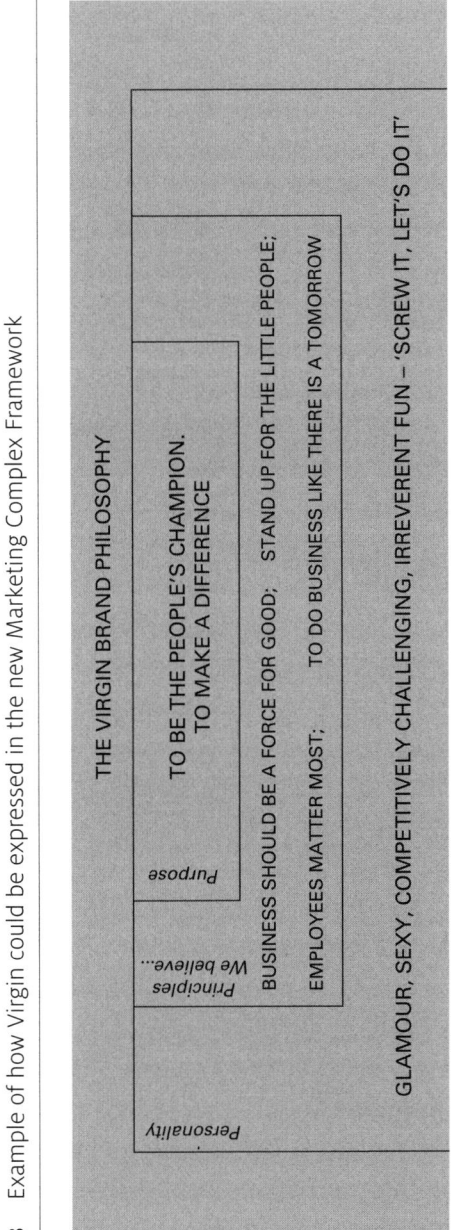

THE VIRGIN BRAND PHILOSOPHY

Personality

Principles
We believe...

Purpose

TO BE THE PEOPLE'S CHAMPION.
TO MAKE A DIFFERENCE

BUSINESS SHOULD BE A FORCE FOR GOOD;   STAND UP FOR THE LITTLE PEOPLE;

EMPLOYEES MATTER MOST;   TO DO BUSINESS LIKE THERE IS A TOMORROW

GLAMOUR, SEXY, COMPETITIVELY CHALLENGING, IRREVERENT FUN – 'SCREW IT, LET'S DO IT'

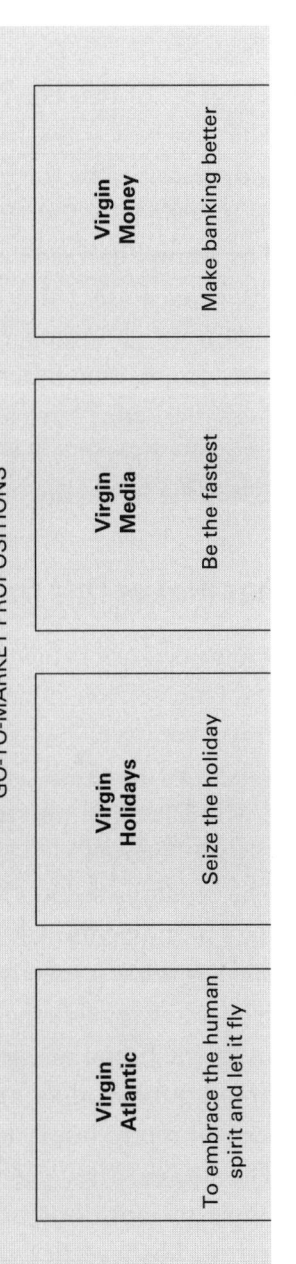

GO-TO-MARKET PROPOSITIONS

Virgin Atlantic	Virgin Holidays	Virgin Media	Virgin Money
To embrace the human spirit and let it fly	Seize the holiday	Be the fastest	Make banking better

In conclusion

Set out above is an alternative to the more traditional brand positioning models – a new framework, the Marketing Complex Framework. It is a 'game of two halves' as they like to say in sports commentary.

The first half is the brand philosophy, the long-term DNA of the brand, described by the brand's purpose, its principles and its personality. It is the branding part of the framework.

The second half isn't actually a single 'thing', other than maybe a multiplicity. Rather it is made up of a variable number of separate propositions, the number of which depends on the brand. Each go-to-market proposition is defined by the target group and the insights the brand's marketers have about them, the benefits the brand offers and the reasons that they are for the target group to believe those promises. It is the marketing 'half' of the framework.

What makes this framework different?

It is a framework rather than a single model, there are now only two parts. One section is entirely flexible and it could, indeed should, change over time.

It is in two sections, which reflects the difference between branding, which is more internally focused, and marketing, which is more externally focused.

The branding section is perhaps surprisingly simpler than many of today's branding models. It has fewer 'sections' to complete, though I would suggest it is merely simplified as much as possible but no more. It deliberately avoids the notion of brand essence and the attempt to simplify the brand in one or two words.

Brand purpose does appear in a number of the brand positioning models of today, but it does not include values.

The second 'half' is primarily different because it allows for multiple propositions, something that current models eschew. It is therefore, I believe, fit for the purpose of managing the true multiplicity of today's brands.

For anyone who has read Collins and Porras's book *Built to Last*, they will recognize a similarity between this framework and a concept that Collins and Porras introduced, namely 'maintain the core and stimulate change'.

Their premise was that a brand needs both to maintain its core philosophy while simultaneously changing the offers it makes as the competitive environment changes, as consumer needs and expectations change, as technology changes or as legislation changes.

The philosophy part of the framework is a means of codifying the core while the go-to-market proposition can change as necessary.

Notes

1 Cool Avenues (2011) [accessed 9 March 2017] Destination Branding [Online] http://www.coolavenues.com/marketing-zone/destination-branding

2 Model (no date) [accessed 13 January 2017] In: *Business Dictionary* [Online] http://www.businessdictionary.com/definition/model.html

3 Kellogg, A (2010) [accessed 13 January 2017] BMW Touts 'Joy,' Value in New Ads, *The Wall Street Journal* [Online] http://www.wsj.com/articles/SB10001424052748704479704575061592413112352

4 GmbH, I (2017) [accessed 13 January 2017] *Joy is BMW*, BMW [Online] http://www.bmw.com.mo/com/en/insights/technology/joy/bmw_joy.html

5 GmbH, I (2017) [accessed 13 January 2017] *Joy is BMW*, BMW [Online] http://www.bmw.com.mo/com/en/insights/technology/joy/bmw_joy.html

The 3Ps of brand 07 philosophy: Purpose, principles and personality

'Follow your passion. It will lead you to your purpose.'
OPRAH WINFREY

On purpose

'To explore strange new worlds, to seek out new life and new civilizations, to boldly go where no man has gone before.'[1]

Star Trek

Clear, inspirational and setting a never-ending goal, the words said first by William Shatner as Captain James T Kirk and subsequently by other captains of the USS *Enterprise* and *Voyager* are a great example of a brand 'purpose'.

The first element of the philosophy of a brand is its purpose, namely the long-term and often never-ending vision that drives the brand. It is the 'dream' that the brand pursues. It is the cause for which the brand campaigns. A good purpose tends to be emotionally led – most often, though not always a poetic and inspirational phrase that at best is short, clear and memorable.

A brand purpose can be likened to planting a flag in the territory the brand wants to own, to champion, to constantly strive for. As such, it is as much an expression of the beliefs of the brand as it is an expression of what it is trying to do for its customers, its consumers, its employees and even for society. It is the territory, the heartland, the concept it wants to align to. A brand purpose should work internally and externally.

A good purpose shows the path forward. It broadens the imagination and, like other good brand purposes, the *Star Trek* example plays a number of roles:

- To guide the brand's strategic direction – to show the path forward.
- To spell out what the brand stands for.
- To energize and mobilize – to tell 'employees' how they should act.

Other good examples of a brand purpose are:

- To make people happy, to create and celebrate a wonderful world of family entertainment – Walt Disney.
- To give ordinary folk the chance to buy the same things as rich people – Wal-Mart.
- To make, distribute and sell the finest quality ice cream and euphoric concoctions with a continued commitment to incorporating wholesome, natural elements and promoting business practices that respect the Earth and the environment – Ben & Jerry's.
- To enable people and businesses throughout the world to realize their full potential – Microsoft.
- To enrich people's lives with programmes and services that inform, educate and entertain – BBC.
- To organize the world's information and make it universally accessible and useful – Google.
- To inspire and nurture the human spirit – one person, one cup, and one neighbourhood at a time – Starbucks.
- To provide a global trading platform where practically anyone can trade practically anything – eBay.

Unfortunately, against the criteria set out above, not all brands' purposes are so well expressed. I think the following could be improved upon:

- [To] produce superior financial returns for its shareowners by providing high value-added logistics, transportation and related business services through focused operating companies. Customer requirements will be met in the highest quality manner appropriate to each market segment served. FedEx will strive to develop mutually rewarding relationships with its team members, partners and suppliers. Safety will be the first consideration in all operations. Corporate activities will be conducted to the highest ethical and professional standards – Fedex.[2]

- [To] aspire to be the leading client-centric global universal bank. We serve shareholders best by putting our clients first and by building a global network of balanced businesses underpinned by strong capital and liquidity. We value our German roots and remain dedicated to our global presence. We commit to a culture that aligns risks and rewards, attracts and develops talented individuals, fosters teamwork and partnership and is sensitive to the society in which we operate – Deutsche Bank.[3]

Compare and contrast the Deutsche Bank example with ING Direct in the United States, which opens with a very clear brand vision and purpose: 'To lead America back to savings'.[4] As the original CEO, Arkadi Kuhlmann, said: 'One way or another, most financial companies are telling you to spend more. We're showing you how to save more'.[5]

Sometimes it may be the need to attract corporate buy-in that causes brands to adopt duller statements. Yahoo's official mission statements have included in the past 'Our mission is to be the most essential global Internet service for consumers and businesses'.[6] Very corporate and, to my mind, very dull.

Since 2007, Yahoo's mission statement has talked about: 'To connect people to their passions, communities, and the world's knowledge'.[7] Better, but perhaps reminiscent of Google's 'To organize the world's information and make it universally accessible and useful'.[8]

Marissa Mayer, when taking up the job as President and CEO, however, did a better job. When asked about what Yahoo did, she said, 'Yahoo is about making the world's daily habits more inspiring and entertaining'.[9]

The website in 2017, however, seems still to be stuck in corporate speak: 'Yahoo is a guide to digital information discovery, focused on informing, connecting, and entertaining through its search, communications, and digital content products'.[10]

As already briefly discussed in Chapter 4, there is a growing belief that the most effective brand purposes are those that express a higher ideal or aim. For advocates of this thinking, a brand purpose can provide a triple win, being good for the brand, representing the right thing to do for the world and humanity and be the best route to corporate growth. While there is a great deal of focus on this in the current marketing press, the idea of an aspirational reason for being, which should inspire an organization, its partners and stakeholders and provide a benefit to local and global society, is not new.

The J&J 'Credo' was written in 1943 and still serves as a statement of the brand's purpose. It is chiselled into the wall of its New Jersey headquarters. It reads:

Our Credo

We believe our first responsibility is to the doctors, nurses and patients, to mothers and fathers and all others who use our products and services. In meeting their needs everything we do must be of high quality. We must constantly strive to reduce our costs in order to maintain reasonable prices. Customers' orders must be serviced promptly and accurately. Our suppliers and distributors must have an opportunity to make a fair profit.

We are responsible to our employees, the men and women who work with us throughout the world. Everyone must be considered as an individual. We must respect their dignity and recognize their merit. They must have a sense of security in their jobs. Compensation must be fair and adequate, and working conditions clean, orderly and safe. We must be mindful of ways to help our employees fulfil their family obligations. Employees must feel free to make suggestions and complaints. There must be equal opportunity for employment, development and advancement for those qualified. We must provide competent management, and their actions must be just and ethical.

We are responsible to the communities in which we live and work and to the world community as well. We must be good citizens – support good works and charities and pay our fair share of taxes. We must encourage civic improvements and better health and education. We must maintain in good order the property we are privileged to use, protecting the environment and natural resources.

> Our final responsibility is to our stockholders. Business must make a sound profit. We must experiment with new ideas. Research must be carried on, innovative programs developed and mistakes paid for. New equipment must be purchased, new facilities provided and new products launched. Reserves must be created to provide for adverse times. When we operate according to these principles, the stockholders should realize a fair return.[11]

The Credo is quoted by Collins and Porras in their 1994 book *Built to Last: Successful habits of visionary companies*[12] and was used to support their analysis, which suggested that organizations whose core purpose isn't profit maximization are, in fact, the most successful long-term companies/brands.

Jim Stengel's 2011 book *Grow: How ideals power growth and profit at the world's greatest companies* supports this contention stating that: 'Evidence suggests that over a 10-year period, businesses with clearly defined and consistently executed brand purposes deliver on average 400% better returns to shareholders'.[13]

Both these books and the analysis in them have been attacked by critics and there is no consensus on the evidence presented. In the EY sponsored *Harvard Business Review* Analytic Services Report, *The Business Case for Brand Purpose*, the conclusion is that:

> 'The global survey of 474 executives found that although there is near-unanimity in the business community about the value of purpose in driving performance, less than half of the executives surveyed said their company had actually articulated a strong sense of purpose and used it as a way to make decisions and strengthen motivation.

> Only a few companies appear to have embedded their purpose to a point where they have reaped its full potential.

> But in those organizations where purpose had become a driver of strategy and decision-making, executives reported a greater ability to deliver revenue growth and drive successful innovation and ongoing transformation'.[14]

There are also a number of highly successful brands that do not have a stated brand purpose. Apple, for example, states its values but has no mission statement on its corporate website.

Other brands have a brand purpose but one that doesn't meet the requirement for a sustainability aspect to their brand, like Brewdog:

> 'We set out on a mission to make other people as passionate about great beer as we are. This promise and premise underpins every single thing we do and acts as a resolute reference point for every single decision we make.'

James Watt (co-founder)[15]

As discussed earlier, unlike marketing, brand purpose more often comes from within rather than from customers and so was the case with British Airways. When faced with challenges and looking to redefine their purpose they found the answer sown into the uniforms of their pilots.

In 2011, BA was in financial trouble, so much so, that it had been losing £1 billion per year. Furthermore, customers were dissatisfied and staff morale was low. Kerris Bright, then Head of Global Marketing, saw the need to reignite the kind of spirit that the organization had previously had. This led to a revitalization programme, a search for what they originally thought would be a new purpose. It started internally – with BA staff.

Bright related the story at The Value Engineers' 2016 'Think Small Play Big' Conference (London 2016):

> 'Despite the challenges, there remained a deep commitment and passion for flying and to fly people better than anybody else. At the heart of everything it [BA] wanted to serve customers in a kind of uniquely special way. It was a group of BA pilots that reminded us that written in their uniforms, on the side of the planes, on their caps it says – 'To Fly. To Serve'. Talking with them, they said "Actually this is why we exist. We know safety and security is important but we exist – To fly, to serve."
>
> So we decided as a marketing-led organization to make that our purpose. At this time of conflict and change, this can be something we can unify behind.
>
> We started [the revitalization programme] inside out and the organization felt really excited, a bit proud and said "yes, this is what we want to be" and then we started to bring that to life for customers'.[16]

Can you have only one purpose?

Currently, there is a generally accepted norm that any purpose or vision should be single-minded and short. While it is undoubtedly true that there are a number of very good brand purpose statements that are both single-minded and succinct, it is equally true to say that there are others that don't conform to this marketing 'urban myth'.

Disney's 'To make people happy'[17] is an example of the former while the BBC's 'To enrich people's lives with programmes and services that inform, educate and entertain'[18] is an example of the latter. The BBC's statement captures the multiplicity of their purpose. They don't just aim to inform people though they do a lot of that via the BBC News network. They don't just educate people though they do everything from educational to factual programmes and they certainly entertain people with the richness and variety of their drama and comedy programmes.

This multiplicity isn't confined to the BBC though. Take Coca-Cola; it also has a three-pronged statement:

- To refresh the world in mind, body and spirit.
- To inspire moments of optimism and happiness through our brands and actions.
- To create value and make a difference.[19]

General Electric's purpose is also multifaceted: 'To invent the next industrial era, to build, move, power and cure the world'.[20]

CASE STUDY

Guinness World Records was born in November 1951 when Sir Hugh Beaver, a keen shot and the then MD of Guinness Breweries, was with a shooting party in the North Slob, on the River Slaney in County Wexford, Ireland. Disappointed at missing a shot, Sir Hugh consoled himself with the fact that the bird in question was a golden plover – the fastest game bird in Europe. At least that is what he thought.

However, a lively debate was soon raging among various members of the party; was the plover actually the fastest game bird or was it the red grouse? The argument continued all the way back to Castlebridge House where the shooting party was staying. Unfortunately, despite an exhaustive search, none of the reference books in the library could confirm which bird was the fastest.

Sir Hugh could have been frustrated, no bird and now no answer, but looking for positives in the negatives, he realized that here was an opportunity. If he and his shooting party were annoyed by the lack of an answer to this one question, how many more unresolved debates were there in the pubs and clubs up and down the land?

Guinness World Records was created originally to be the provider of definitive answers but soon also became the inspirer of other world-record breaking attempts. Today this dual role is reflected on its website where it defines its purpose as:

'We inspire people – individuals, families, schools, teams, groups, companies and communities – of any age, in any city or country.

We want that inspiration to come from reading, watching, listening to and participating in record breaking.

We don't define or recognise success in a conventional or limited way and so draw upon the entire range of superlatives to help people realise their potential and to re-examine the world.'[21]

But it goes on to define its vision as 'To make the amazing official' and its mission as 'To be the ultimate global authority on record breaking'. Its current tagline 'Officially Amazing' further sums up the duality of the brand's purpose, which on the one hand is the official measuring, documenting and authorizing of world records while on the other hand it has a role to champion the inspiration and enjoyment of those records.

Purpose, vision and mission

Before moving on from brand purpose to principles, a final and important distinction needs to be made between a brand purpose and a business mission. A business mission is a strategic, goal-orientated statement of what the brand's business objectives are, what it aims to achieve. Business missions tend to be more functional and often include specific targets against set timelines.

The two classic examples of business missions are 'To become the world's number 1/best/leading/most respected entertainment/

transportation/technology company' and 'To be a $X billion company by 2025'. The most used variation on this just combines the two: 'To reach $X billion in revenue and become one of the world's top five brands by 2020'.

The brand purpose and the business mission should work together. The purpose sets the long-term core vision for the brand while the business mission outlines the company's plan and sets specific measurable goals.

Diagrammatically this can be shown as in Figure 7.1. The business mission relates more to current business models and the brand purpose relates to the philosophy and longer-term vision. The yin and yang of the organization.

Figure 7.1 How business missions and brand purpose fit together to form the overall organization strategy

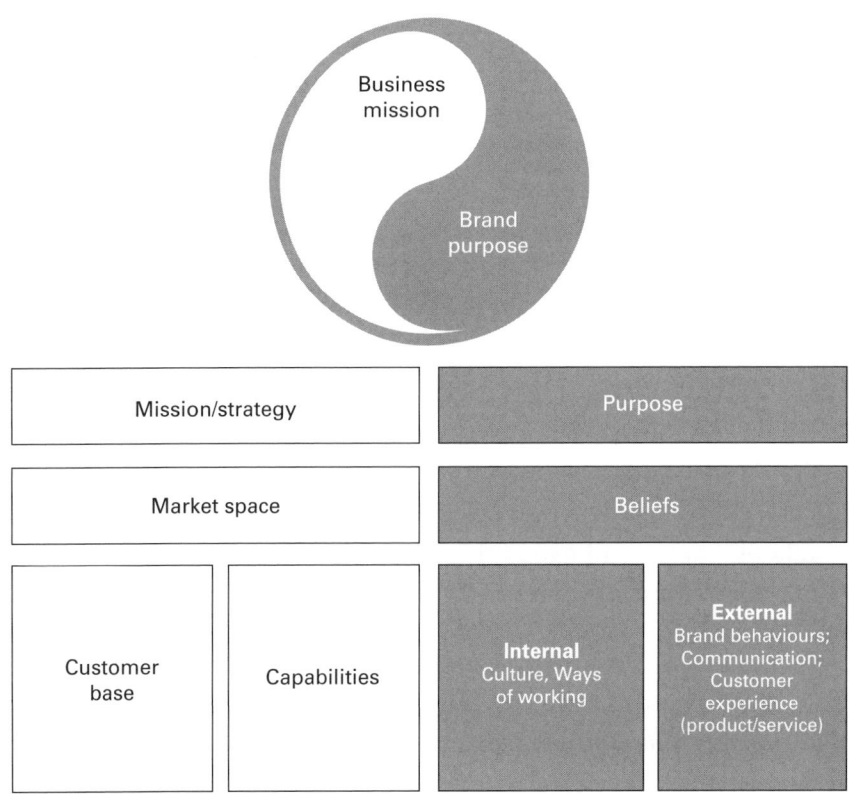

SOURCE The Value Engineers

On principle

Values have been devalued.

Too often, when given the option to define a brand's values, marketers default to the easy and now overused single-word answers – caring, integrity, innovative. These and other words like them fail to do what they are supposed to do; namely, help shape what a brand does and set the parameters for how it wants to behave. As a result, the current practice of defining and expressing brand values seems to be leading to a blandness not brand-ness in brand positioning.

How often have you seen the same words stated over and over as brand values? If, like me, you have done the analysis you will know the same words are used frequently, very frequently.

Following the publication of Interbrand's 2014 most valuable brands, my colleagues at The Value Engineers and I decided to look more closely at the values of these valuable brands. Our analysis shows that the values these brands ascribe to are a pretty predictable bunch. Many are worthy table-stakes for any reputable company yet there is little differentiation in them.

Of the 100 brands listed we found published brand values for 53 of them, and the average number of values they each had was five (Figure 7.2). The distinction of being the company with the most values went to Allianz, who had nine. There were a total of 35 values, with the five highest ranked being 'Caring about People' (51 per cent), 'Integrity' (49 per cent), 'Innovative' (45 per cent) 'Collaboration' (40 per cent) and 'Quality' (36 per cent). [22]

Of the 35 values, 21 were used by more than one brand, and perhaps not surprisingly the top-rated values appear in almost all of the brands. In fact, one brand (UPS) claimed the Brand Values bingo 'full house' having all five of the top five values.

Looking more closely at the values, a number of subgroups emerged:

- 'Respectful' Qualities – Caring about People, Integrity and Respect.
- 'Company' Qualities – Dedication, Quality, Professionalism and Consistency.

Figure 7.2 Percentage of brands claiming to a have a specific value

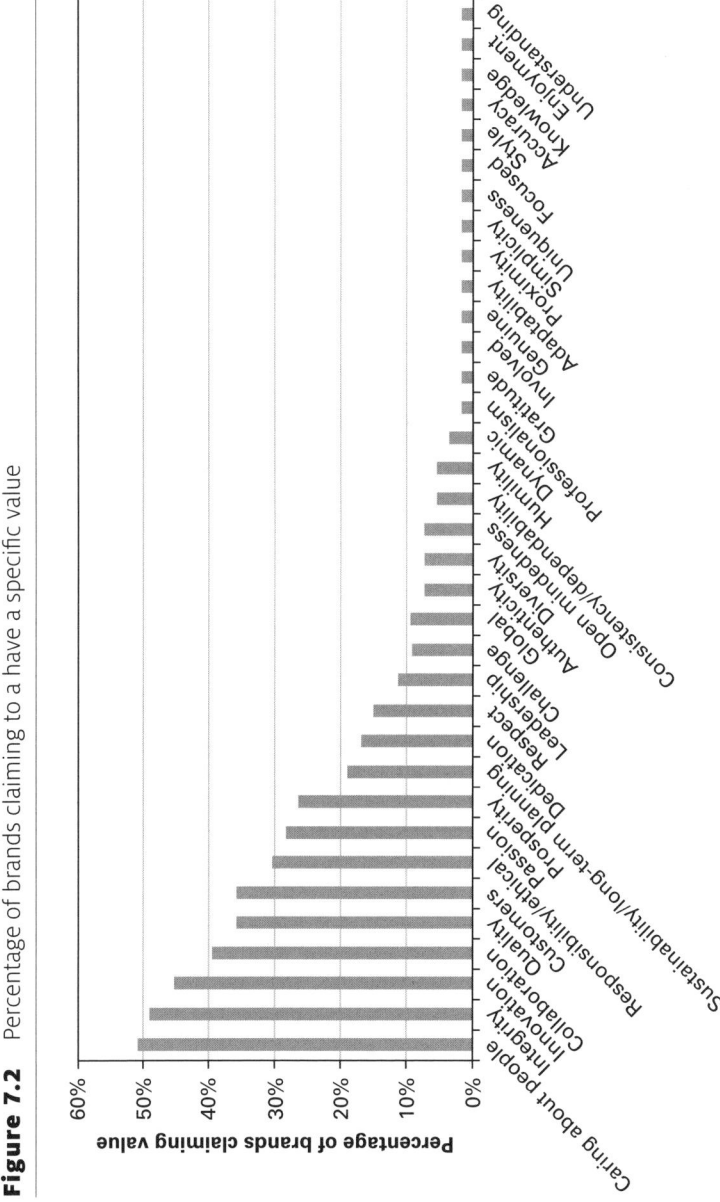

SOURCE The Value Engineers' analysis of brand websites (2017)

- 'Global' Qualities – Sustainability, Responsibility, Global, Diversity and Adaptability.
- 'Teamwork' Qualities – Collaboration, Customers, Proximity and Involved.
- 'Human' Qualities – Genuine, Gratitude, Humility, Open Mindedness, Enjoyment and Understanding.
- Ambitious Qualities – Innovation, Prosperity, Leadership, Being Challenging, Passion and Focused.

When re-plotted further the values showed the preference and concentration around respectfulness, teamwork and ambition (Figure 7.3).[23]

Now it is classical marketing theory that:

1 Brands define the 'DNA' of an organization.

2 Brands need to be differentiated, or at least distinctive.

3 Values are the building blocks of a brand's DNA.

However, what our analysis seemed to show was that too many brands aren't differentiating themselves well enough. One of the reasons appeared to be that when selecting values, marketers are choosing the 'motherhood' and 'apple pie' values – values which everyone can agree to; values which are 'table-stakes' but not really differentiating.

Another problem with values is the way that they are often expressed in organizations; without naming names, I once worked with a client who said they had 'teamwork' as a core value. They depicted this with the image of a skydiving team all holding hands and superimposed the word 'Teamwork'. Needless to say it did little to help them or their employees.

The value of values is when they help either define and differentiate brands, or when they help people internally know how to behave and externally know what to expect from a brand. When they are chosen and depicted like this, they are almost valueless.

It is for a combination of these reasons that we prefer to use beliefs or principles when defining a brand and its philosophy. One recent example comes from working with Convergence Group, a network

Figure 7.3 Percentage of brands claiming to have a specific value clustered by type of value

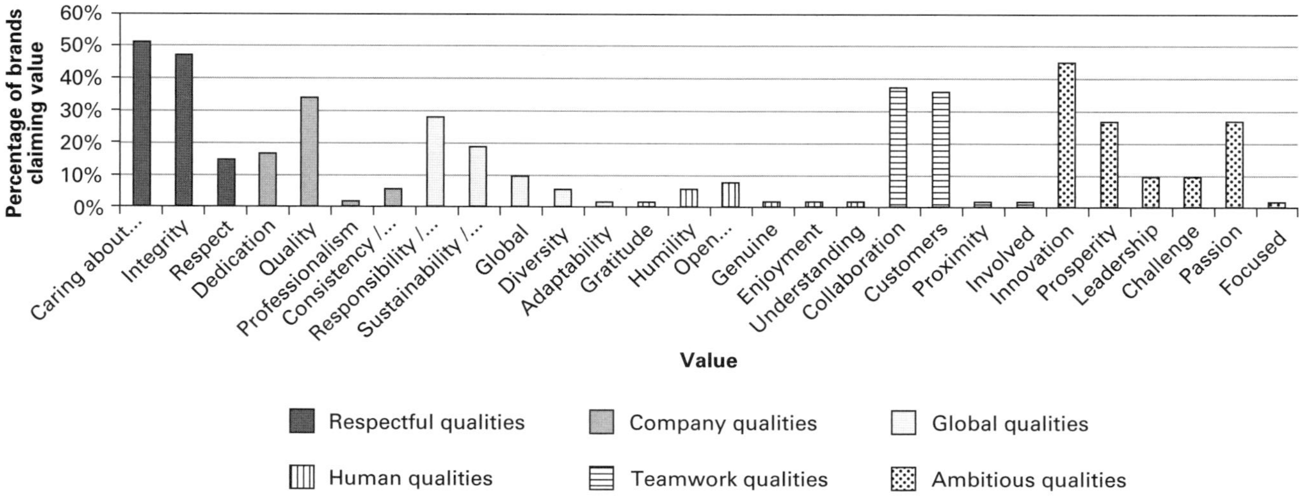

SOURCE The Value Engineers' analysis of brand websites (2017)

service provider in the United Kingdom, led by the charismatic MD Neal Harrison. Harrison is personally an advocate of what has become one of the brand principles of the Convergence Group, the 'Ask Once' principle.

He identified a software industry problem, though many will recognize it from just about any service industry. The problem that so many customers face is being passed from department to department, from person to person, and never finding someone to listen and, therefore, never getting an answer.

'Ask once' is Harrison's antidote. He insists that whoever takes the call, takes the responsibility. A customer should only have to ask once and whoever they have asked needs to find the answer and get back to the customer even if the answer may be 'No'. The customer shouldn't need to ask again.

It's a great example of why a principle is better than a value. The value might have been 'responsible', which has all the issues of blandness and vagueness, while 'Ask once' is clear and directional. It lets the customer know what to expect and sets behaviour guidelines for employees.

Another great example comes from Apple. This brand is famous for not publishing its purpose or mission statement but is a brand that has a clear and distinct persona.

In one of Apple's (AAPL) conference calls with investors in January 2009, Tim Cook outlined a number of the brand's core beliefs:

'We *believe* we're on the face of the Earth to make great products.

We *believe* in the simple, not the complex.

We *believe* in saying no to thousands of projects, so that we can really focus. We *believe* in deep collaboration and cross-pollinization of our groups.' [my italics][24]

Other beliefs Cook mentioned included their unwillingness to settle for anything less than excellence in everything they do throughout the company, the honesty and humility to admit when they are wrong, and the courage to change and make things better. Now, he did go and ruin it by actually calling them 'values', but as you can see they are not the one-word banalities that are usually called values. They have more richness and personality to them; they impact on behaviours and customer expectations.

Cook then went on to describe how these beliefs were more than just words and are regularly seen in the brand's actions. One example he used related to a problem they had in Asia. He and his team, which included Sabih Khan – a key operations manager, decided something had to be done. Khan is reported to have stood up, left the meeting, driven straight to the airport and without even a change of clothes booked himself onto an open-ended flight to China so he could start sorting the problem as soon as possible.

It also highlights another side and benefit of true beliefs or principles – a principle isn't a principle until it costs you money. It's too easy for brands to 'sign up' to loose values that are difficult to measure, but if they express their beliefs they have something to live up to and be measured by. If a brand has a true principle it is something to which it is willing to stick, even if it means it is more expensive to do or it closes down an opportunity.

For example, one of the Disney brand's principles is that everything it does under the Disney brand name should be suitable for all the family. That means that while it has the resources and capabilities to produce films, which would appeal to an older adult audience if the certification was such that they could only be seen by adults, the Disney brand wouldn't make them.

However, the business gets around this by making films such as *Pretty Woman* and *Good Morning, Vietnam* but doesn't make or market them under the Disney name. It also explains why the 'Disney' distribution company is branded Buena Vista and not Disney.

Moving forward, marketers need to consider that the capturing of a brand's DNA isn't just a job of cataloguing the easy 95 per cent. They need to define and express the whole brand in distinctive and practical terms, and to do so they need to recognize that the value of values is limited, whereas it is my belief that the power of beliefs and principles is much greater.

A financial organization already given honourable mention for its stated purpose but which also has a well-defined set of principles is

ING Direct (USA). ING Direct was launched in September 2000. It is an internet based savings bank, dealing directly with its customers.

In line with its purpose, 'To lead America back to savings', it believes its role is to encourage savings not spending. 'One way or another, most financial companies are telling you to spend more. We're showing you how to save more,' said CEO and chief brand manager, Arkadi Kuhlmann.[25]

So ING Direct doesn't market credit cards, doesn't offer checking/current accounts or provide auto loans – all products that make many of its competitors lots of money!

The 'innocent' brand in the UK was one of the pioneers of the fruit smoothie market, and has a stated principle of never using fruit concentrates. As the market has become more competitive it is a principle that has, and will, cost the brand money but it is one that it believes in and so is sticking to it.

Practically speaking, we recommend drafting beliefs principles as full sentences starting 'We believe…' as this helps avoid the danger of clichéd one-word 'values' creeping back in. However, sometimes you can learn as much from examples of what you shouldn't do, as you learn from positive examples like those quoted above.

Kendra Eash's 'The Generic Brand Video'[26] originally posted on Timothy McSweeney's Internet Tendency is a wonderful, satirical and insightful pastiche of the bland corporate brand video. If you haven't read it, you should. It's a great example of what not to do.

It begins:

'We think first
Of vague words that are synonyms for progress
And pair them with footage of a high-speed train.

Science
Is doing lots of stuff
That may or may not have anything to do with us.
See how this guy in a lab coat holds up a beaker?
That means we do research.
Here's a picture of DNA.

> There are a shitload of people in the world
> Especially in India
> See how we're part of the global economy?
> Look at these farmers in China.'

And continues in similar style.

If you prefer to watch, look up the video that Dissolve made based on Eash's piece.[27]

Personality

The brand personality is traditionally a section of any brand framework, whereas the name suggests the brand is personified. It is an attempt to describe the brand as if it was human. How it would behave. Its attitudes, its personality and how it would interact with others. The aim of the box is to define the brand's character, style and tone of voice.

Not surprisingly, words like 'caring' and 'innovative' readily and frequently spring to marketers' minds. Heard those before? Interestingly, this has led to the many debates about the differences between values and personality in models where they are both used. It is perhaps another reason why replacing values with principles can help marketing teams better define their brands. If and when completed well, the personality of any brand definition can be important in defining the brand's USP – not the classic 'Unique Selling Proposition' of the 1950s but rather the 'Unique Selling Persona' discussed earlier.

'T'ain't what you do (It's the way that you do it)' is a song written by jazz musicians Melvin 'Sy' Oliver and James 'Trummy' Young. Jimmie Lunceford, Harry James and Ella Fitzgerald first recorded it in 1939.[28] It was turned into a ska-style pop song with the slightly altered title of 'It ain't what you do...' and recorded by Fun Boy Three and Bananarama in 1981. Released in 1982, it became a big hit in the United Kingdom, reaching number four in the singles chart.[29] It could be the theme tune for this, the third and final, part of the core brand philosophy, as the lyrics provide guidance for marketers: 'It ain't what you do but the way that you do it, that's what gets results'.[30]

In an era where technology allows rivals to copy what a brand does, it is no longer what you do that distinguishes brands. It is the way you do it – the style and manner in which a specific brand acts and expresses itself is what creates a real point of distinctiveness. Many brands offer similar products and services, and often there is limited physical difference between them but the style and tone of voice with which they are delivered and marketed is, in fact, what differentiates them.

It has been said to me that British Airways was the first airline to introduce the fully reclining seat. Singapore Airways soon followed adding a duvet rather than blanket, and Virgin followed that with the first fully reclining double seat and the inference of a better way of joining the mile high club!

The brand personality is a definition of how a brand behaves, what its attitude and culture is. Tropicana and innocent both produce 100 per cent orange juice but the real difference between the two is less physical and more a matter of personality. On their website in January 2017 Tropicana promised 'Tropicana for Health' and went on to describe their orange juice as 'Our classic Tropicana Pure Premium orange juice, with one and a half oranges in every glass. As delicious today as it's ever been'.[31] On the same day, innocent on their website said, 'Laugh in the face of Winter' and described their orange juice as: 'This is our most popular recipe. No peel, no bits, just the smoothest and tastiest juice we've ever made, in a smart carafe. We hope it brightens up your breakfast'.[32]

ING Direct describes its personality and culture as 'Main Street, not Wall Street'.[33] It therefore aims to treat all its customers the same way – so there is no special treatment for larger savers and no minimum deposit. It doesn't want to be another 'boring' financial company and deliberately recruits people who don't have previous financial company experience.

Visit the Lurpak website, read the copy, watch the ads and enjoy the cooking demonstrations and you'll soon see that though they, like many other brands, champion cooking, they do it with a strong and distinctive feel, a tone of voice and distinctive photographic style:

'Cooks, you know exactly what to do in the kitchen without scrolling through your feeds. Watching cookery shows can't compare to the thrill of flame-grilling a steak, the feeling of dough between your fingers and the smell of mackerel sizzling in melted butter.

So get that apron out, turn the TV off and turn the oven on... it's time to let out the cook in you'.[34]

In a conversation with Matt Close when he was global brand director for Axe/Lynx, the Unilever personal care brand, he described how he, mimicking the scene in *The Matrix*, would offer new team members the red or the blue pill, testing their resolve to adopt the style and culture of the Lynx brand team. He puts this unity of understanding and purpose as one of the reasons the brand is so successful.

When more can be less

Looking at many brand positioning statements over the years, it is clear that there is a tendency, a desire even, to distil things down to a single word. It is a laudable wish but one which can again lead to misunderstanding through oversimplification.

An ex-colleague of mine, Lou Ellerton, set a short exercise when working with a client to help define a brand personality. She asked them to put down what three different brand personality traits meant to them and how they depict them. First up was the word 'Fun' – which drew ideas from bouncy castles and custard pies to a range of famous comedians. 'British' prompted thoughts ranging from Winston Churchill to punk rockers. 'Irreverent' drew up notions of challenging conventions and the US show *SNL*. Then, she asked people to do the same exercise for 'Irreverent, British Fun'; the results were amazingly consistent.

Sometimes more can be less – more words, less confusion. We recommend that when looking at defining or personality, using two words together can be better than one, and the second or third word can often be an adjective or qualifier of the first. When defining the culture of The Value Engineers, we describe ourselves not as 'challenging' but as 'constructively challenging'. For us, it's not enough just to be able to ask difficult questions; we want to be able to have at least one or part of an answer too!

Working with a service brand recently, the word 'generous' was suggested as a personality trait. For some this meant generosity in the sense of giving more (ideally for less) so was tied with size and value. For others it meant generous in terms of attention, interest, openness and a willingness to extend to others what they would want for themselves. After a discussion, the team agreed that the latter was what they were trying to capture, and in the end used the term 'Generosity of Spirit'.

As mentioned earlier, a traditional personality box often carries the instruction to the team compiling it to use it 'to describe the brand as if it was a person'. On the face of it, this can seem logical but it is worth noting some of the limitations that this brings with it.

Firstly, there is a danger of groupthink and who is popular at any given time. If the brand is to be described as a person everyone using that description needs to know who that person is and what his or her personality is. This narrows the pool of possibilities down. Then popularity tends to mean that certain people within this pool are more top-of-mind and more favourably perceived, which further narrows the options. Consequently, over the years it has been possible to see cycles when one or two names would recur with alarming frequency. Michael Palin, Tom Hanks, Brian Cox and Nigella Lawson are among the names I have seen most often.

The other weakness with this approach is that brands are increasingly global and many of the personification values that feel just right in one country don't travel well or far enough. I had a client who felt their brand personality should be like James Corden but realized that in over half the countries in which the brand was present people would have no idea who he was.

In conclusion

It was E Jerome McCarthy, in his 1960 book *Basic Marketing: A managerial approach*, who first distilled the concept of the marketing mix down to the 4Ps – product, pricing, place and promotion.

The first section of the new framework pays homage to this alliteration but suggests a different set of Ps to define a different idea, namely the brand philosophy, which is perhaps the fifth P.

The choice of the word philosophy is deliberate. It aims to differentiate this approach from 'positioning', which we have seen can and does have multiple meanings and uses in a brand and marketing context – market positioning, needs positioning and brand positioning. The framework also reflects the dictionary definition of (a) philosophy, namely: 'A theory or attitude that acts as a guiding principle for behaviour'.[35]

In this context a brand philosophy is based on:

- A clear and well-defined purpose, which increasingly is the reason 'why' you exist beyond the desire to make profit.

- A set of principles: fundamental beliefs that shape what a brand stands for and how it behaves.

- A personality that describes the way in which the brand behaves in relation to all its different stakeholder groups.

Notes

1 *Star Trek* (1966) [TV series] Norway Productions, Gene Roddenberry

2 Investors.fedex.com (2017) [accessed 16 January 2017] Mission & Goals, *FedEx* [Online] http://investors.fedex.com/company-overview/mission-and-goals/default.aspx

3 Db.com (2017) [accessed 31 May 2017] Vision and Brand, *Deutsche Bank* [Online] https://annualreport.deutsche-bank.com/2014/ar/deutsche-bank-group.html

4 Reiss, R (2009) [accessed 16 January 2017] Creating a New Kind of Savings Bank, *Forbes* [Online] http://www.forbes.com/2009/12/01/kuhlmann-ing-direct-leadership-managing-banking.html

5 Reiss, R (2009) [accessed 16 January 2017] Creating a New Kind of Savings Bank, *Forbes* [Online] http://www.forbes.com/2009/12/01/kuhlmann-ing-direct-leadership-managing-banking.html

6 Info.yahoo.com (2017) [accessed 16 January 2017] Yahoo Terms of Service, *Yahoo! UK Terms Centre* [Online] http://info.yahoo.com/legal/uk/yahoo/cop/en-gb/details.html

7 Russell, T (2007) [accessed 16 January 2017] Yahoo's New Mission: Making Us Mingle, *Wired* [Online] Available at: https://www.wired.com/2007/05/yahoos_new_miss/

8 Russell, T (2007) Yahoo's New Mission: Making Us Mingle, *Wired* [Online] https://www.wired.com/2007/05/yahoos_new_miss/

9 CNN (2017) [accessed 16 January 2017] *30 Minutes with Marissa Mayer* [Online] http://money.cnn.com/video/technology/enterprise/2012/11/28/t-marissa-mayer-yahoo-ceo.fortune/index.html

10 Yahoo (2017) [accessed 16 January 2017] About Yahoo [Online] https://about.yahoo.com/

11 Johnson & Johnson (2017) [accessed 16 January 2017] *Our Credo/Johnson & Johnson* [Online] Available at: https://www.jnj.com/about-jnj/jnj-credo

12 Collins, J and Porras, J (2000) *Built to Last: Successful habits of visionary companies*, 3rd edn, Random House, London

13 Stengel, J (2011) *Grow: How ideals power growth and profit at the world's greatest companies*, 1st edn, Crown Business, New York

14 EY Beacon Institute (2017) [accessed 12 January 2017] The Business Case for Purpose, *Harvard Business Review* [Online] http://www.ey.com/Publication/vwLUAssets/ey-the-business-case-for-purpose/$FILE/ey-the-business-case-for-purpose.pdf

15 Watt, J (2015) *Business for Punks: Break all the rules – the BrewDog way*, 1st edn, Portfolio, Penguin, London

16 Bright, K (2017) [accessed 26 January 2017] Think Small Play Big Conference, London, The Value Engineers [Online] https://www.thevalueengineers.com/company-news/think-small-play-big/important-staying-true-purpose-thinksmall

17 Disney UK (2017) [accessed 16 January 2017] The Official Home For All Things Disney, *Disney UK* [Online] http://disney.co.uk/

18 BBC (2017) [accessed 16 January 2017] Mission and Values – Inside the BBC, *BBC* [Online] http://www.bbc.co.uk/aboutthebbc/insidethebbc/whoweare/mission_and_values

19 Coca-Cola (2017) [accessed 16 January 2017] Our Mission Statement & Company Values, *Coca-Cola GB* [Online] http://www.coca-cola.co.uk/about-us/mission-vision-and-values

20 GE (2014) [accessed 9 March 2017] Annual Report (2014), Atlanta, GA, USA [Online] https://www.ge.com/ar2014/ceo-letter/

21 Guinness World Records (2017) [accessed 16 January 2017] About Guinness World Records [Online] http://www.guinnessworldrecords.com/corporate

22 Lury, G (2016) Brand-ness or blandness? Why I believe in beliefs and don't value values, *Market Leader* (Quarter 1)

23 Lury, G (2016) Brand-ness or blandness? Why I believe in beliefs and don't value values, *Market Leader* (Quarter 1)

24 Lashinsky, A (2009) [accessed 18 January 2017] The Cook Doctrine at Apple, *Fortune* [Online] http://fortune.com/2009/01/22/the-cook-doctrine-at-apple/

25 Reiss, R (2009) [accessed 16 January 2017] Creating a New Kind of Savings Bank, *Forbes* [Online] http://www.forbes.com/2009/12/01/kuhlmann-ing-direct-leadership-managing-banking.html

26 Eash, K (2017) [accessed 16 January 2017] This is a Generic Brand Video, *McSweeney's Internet Tendency* [Online] https://www.mcsweeneys.net/articles/this-is-a-generic-brand-video

27 *This is a Generic Brand Video* (2017) [accessed 16 January 2017] [video] Dissolve [Online] https://www.youtube.com/watch?v=2YBtspm8j8M

28 Oliver, M, Young, J, Lunceford, J, James, H and Fitzgerald, E (1939) *T'ain't what you do (It's the way that you do it)* [Radio] Decca Records, New York

29 Fun Boy Three and Bananarama (1982) *It ain't what you do* [7-inch single and 12-inch single vinyl] Chrysalis Records, UK

30 Fun Boy Three and Bananarama (1982) *It ain't what you do* [7-inch single and 12-inch single vinyl] Chrysalis Records, UK

31 Tropicana (2017) [accessed 16 January 2017] Orange Products, *Tropicana UK* [Online] https://www.tropicana.co.uk/our-products/orange

32 innocent (2017) [accessed 16 January 2017] *Things we make – Juices – Smooth orange juice* [Online] https://www.innocentdrinks.co.uk/things-we-make/juices/juice/smooth-orange-juice

33 Customer World (2008) [accessed 18 January 2017] *Learning Customer-centricity from ING Direct* [Online] http://customerworld.typepad.com/swami_weblog/2008/11/learning-customercentricity-from-ing-direct.html

34 Lurpak (2017) [accessed 10 March 2017] Game On, Cooks, *Lurpak* [Online] http://www.lurpak.co.uk/game-on-cooks/

35 Philosophy (2017) [accessed 16 January 2017] In: *Oxford Dictionary*, Oxford University Press, Oxford [Online] https://en.oxforddictionaries.com/definition/philosophy

Going to market: Brand propositions

'I'm going to make him an offer he can't refuse.'
DON VITO CORLEONE (IN THE BOOK, AND SUBSEQUENTLY
THE MOVIE, *THE GODFATHER*, BOTH WRITTEN BY MARIO PUZO)

How would you sell a rainbow?

Figure 8.1

SOURCE Pexels image

'If I was trying to sell a rainbow to a customer I would tell them about its natural beauty and ability to inspire.

If I was trying to sell rainbows to schools as an educational device, I would talk about prisms and the refraction of light.

If I was asking someone to join me in creating rainbows I might give them a set of seven colours: red, orange, yellow, green, blue, indigo and violet, and see what they could do.

If I was trying to sell my rainbow brand to some investors, I would tell them about the pot of gold at its end.'

This is an example I use to help explain the second section of the new multipart Marketing Complex Framework and the need for the multiple go-to-market propositions, with the emphasis on multiple and the 's' on the end of propositions.

It is an easy-to-understand demonstration of one of the key differences and the key benefits of the new framework, namely that it recognizes and facilitates the inclusion of multiple propositions. This works whether those different propositions are for one product or service engaging with multiple stakeholders as in this case or in instances where one brand may offer a range of different products and services; for example, if brand was about weather-ness and I also promoted wind and snow.

Using the new framework it is possible to have propositions for each product or service or, indeed, multiple propositions for the multiple products and services where they have a variety of target groups and stakeholders.

The aim of the framework was to create a structure that can manage complexity while providing coherency and not resorting to bland one-size-fits-all consistency. As the rainbow example shows, each proposition is shaped by the brand philosophy but tailored to the specific target or stakeholder group. The philosophy acts as a 'lens' through which all the propositions should be seen. It is this lens and its application that provides that coherency.

Going to market

Often attributed to Nelson Mandela but actually first said by Joel Barker, a futurist and filmmaker, in the training video *The Power of Vision*, the notion that 'Thinking without action is only dreaming, action without thinking is only passing time but thinking and action combined can change the world' links to the two halves of the framework.[1]

The brand philosophy is in many ways the 'thinking' in Barker's quote. It sets out the overall direction, the 'dream' of the brand and some parameters about what the brand should and shouldn't do. The go-to-market propositions are more aligned to the 'actions'. These are the expressions of the offers, the promises, the interactions and the brand encounters, and when done together they can change sectors. They can change markets. They can change the world.

Traditionally, there are different types of brand propositions – consumer proposition, customer value proposition and employee value proposition:

- **Consumer proposition**

  Definition: A succinct statement of the benefits being offered to a specific and identified target audience by a company or by a specific product or service. The 'original' proposition and the one that is the focus in most existing brand models.

  Focus: B2C (business to consumer)

- **Customer value proposition**

  Definition: The offer that one company or brand makes to its clients/customers to help them derive or create better value (either by helping them cut their costs or by helping them create greater value). A variation on the consumer proposition and tailored to a business-to-business market, which is generally seen to be more functionally led, hence the increased emphasis on value, whether that be value added or costs saved.

  Focus: B2B (business to business) or B2B2C (business to business to consumer)

- **Employee value proposition**

  Definition: A statement of the benefits that an employer is offering to its employees to attract and retain them. Another variation this time reflecting the role of brands internally and as a factor in talent attraction.

  Focus: B2E (Business to employee – potential or existing)

Given that there are different definitions here, this might suggest that marketers do already deal in multiplicity and in some cases that is undoubtedly true. However, in many other cases marketers still focus on developing their proposition (singular) depending on whether it is a B2C or a B2B brand. Whether or not there is a B2E proposition and how closely it is aligned to any overall brand positioning and proposition varies enormously. In many cases, it is developed independently by the HR or Talent management team (though this is changing and becoming more aligned).

As discussed earlier a proposition of any type traditionally includes four or five elements:

1 **A frame of reference** – What market or sector is the brand competing in? How does the target group see and define this cluster?

2 **The target group** – Who are you targeting/engaging? Who are they? They can be described demographically, attitudinally or behaviourally.

3 **Insight** – An insight is generally defined as a penetrating understanding that gets to the real needs and motivations of the consumer target, and therefore identifies or suggests a business opportunity. They can alternatively and more simply be defined as an 'Aha-Kerching!' An insight is a combination of an 'Aha' moment of revelation that can be translated in a business idea that will help make the cash registers ring – Kerching!

   This is where market research can play a major role in helping to identify the tensions that people are facing. These are the tensions that products can help address, providing solutions. For example, many people wish they could prepare more homemade meals but don't have the time to do so, especially during the week. A good insight helps suggest the benefit or a product that people would be interested in.

4 The benefit/The promise – What's in it for them? This is the crux of any proposition – hopefully this is an expression of an offer they can't refuse. Here there is an important distinction between a feature and a benefit, perhaps best understood using a quote from the Harvard marketing professor, Theodore Levitt, who said: 'People don't want to buy a quarter-inch drill. They want a quarter-inch hole'. This quote does a great job in making the distinction between a product or feature and a benefit and is used frequently by marketers, consultants and marketing academics around the world.

However, in truth it probably needs to be taken a stage further. Does the person buying the drill and drill bits really just want holes, or do they want something more? Do they want to put up shelves easily and conveniently? Do they want to feel that they are a bit of a handyperson and demonstrate this to their spouse, family and friends? Do they want to save the money that it would have cost them to get someone in to do their odd jobs around the house?

One way of thinking about this is a benefit ladder (Figure 8.2).

Figure 8.2   The benefit ladder – a model for exploring the benefit of the benefit

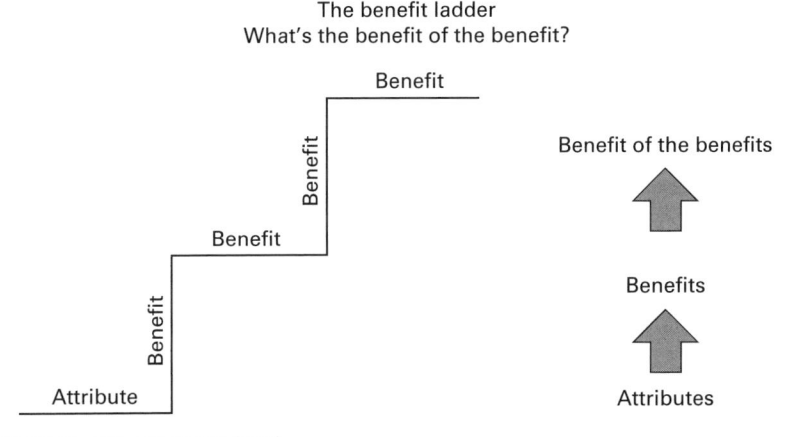

SOURCE The Value Engineers (2017)

CASE STUDY Unilever and Persil/Omo

Taking Unilever's Persil/Omo detergent as an example, it is possible to see how their 'Dirt is good' proposition comes several rungs up a benefit ladder. (Unilever uses different brand names in different countries – Persil in the UK and Omo in Europe.)

Persil/Omo detergent:

- Gives me really effective cleaning.
- It cleans even the tough stains that children get on their clothes (through their natural desire to explore and get dirty).
- So I have the confidence that even when they get really dirty, Persil/Omo will get their clothes clean again.
- I'm free to let my children enjoy the fun of getting dirty.
- I feel like a good parent.

It was also a proposition that connected to a deep insight that the Unilever team had uncovered, and which resonated with its customers: 'If you are not free to get dirty, you cannot experience life and grow'.

As David Arkwright, the former global brand director for Unilever's laundry business, said in a feature he wrote for *Campaign* magazine, they now had the basis for a new narrative that: 'dirt equates to creativity; and parents aspire to have creative, free-thinking and playing kids, as opposed to those locked into pristine-clean conformity.'[2]

Launched in 2008, the Dirt is Good proposition has been very successful helping drive brand growth. 'By the end of 2009, (Dirt is Good) DIG's double-digit growth and market share gains in key markets had contributed positively to Unilever's overall performance and made DIG one of Unilever's largest global brands.'[3]

Another take on the difference between product/feature and benefit comes in an equally famous but somewhat politically incorrect quote from Charles Revson, the founder of Revlon. He said: 'In the factory we make cosmetics. In the store we sell hope,' which again highlights the distinction but perhaps more strongly emphasizes the difference between a rational product feature and an emotional end benefit. This can be seen in the Persil/Omo example where the laddering up of benefits include both functional (cleans even the tough stains) through to the confidence and the feeling of being a good parent.

A final point on the proposition or promise relates to the notion of overpromising and under-delivering. A great proposition may encourage people to buy or use your product and so the temptation is to promise as much as you can... and sometimes more. However, there is an inherent danger in this approach. If the product or service does not deliver against that promise, this may be the quickest way to kill that product or service and to damage the brand as well. Not only will people feel cheated by the performance of the product or service and be unlikely to buy it again, they will also lose trust in the brand. This is why the best brands don't just think of propositions as promises but as responsibilities.

5 **Reasons to believe** – Why should the target group believe what you are promising them? What evidence or proof points exist? What assertions can you make about the brand that will support your proposition? What actions of the brand help to substantiate the promise it makes?

This can range from hard scientific evidence, the (in)famous proof from market research 'Eight out of ten cats...' to softer, more inferred 'proofs'. These include being number 1/market leader (you must be good), in business since 1849 (so we have built up our expertise) to elements that might suggest a logic. When Tetley teabags in the United Kingdom changed from square to round, their 'proof' that this might make a better cup of tea was that by being round they fitted your mug better. Not the most scientific proof but the change was a huge success for them.

A well-known and used model that pulls these elements together is shown in Figure 8.3. It provides a framework in which positions can be developed and easily expressed.

Its one possible weakness is that in use there is still a tendency to look for a single-minded proposition, which is in reality just another form of the USP.

Figure 8.3 Simplified proposition framework

```
┌─────────────────────────────────────────────────────────┐
│                                                           │
│   For  ...........................(TARGET AUDIENCE).........................  │
│                                                           │
│   is the  .........................(FRAME OF REFERENCE) ..................  │
│                                                           │
│   that offers .................. (PROPOSITION/BENEFITS) ................  │
│                                                           │
│   because.......................(REASONS TO BELIEVE)..................  │
│                                                           │
└─────────────────────────────────────────────────────────┘
```

SOURCE The Value Engineers (2017)

Single-minded propositions

In keeping with the notion of simplifying as much as possible but no more, it is worth mentioning that the prevailing mantra is that propositions need to be single-minded. However, history and common sense suggest that this isn't always the case. 'Helps you work, rest and play': the famous proposition for a Mars bar is an obvious example, which seems to be conveniently forgotten when singularity is being proposed.

Recently, Unilever announced that it was renaming its 'I Can't Believe It's Not Butter' spread to 'I Can't Believe It's So Good… For Everything'. A new design has therefore been developed. Interestingly, its own public statement recognizes that it wants to communicate a multifaceted proposition. 'The company said the revamped name will help to "engage a new audience by highlighting the versatility, great taste and health benefits of the spread".'[4]

Powerful propositions

The same mantra about the importance of getting the actual expression right, which was discussed earlier, is also very true for propositions. It ain't just what you say, it's the way that you say it… and how you execute it that drives sales.

Figure 8.4   Nurofen brand logo complementing the targeted pain proposition

SOURCE Reckitt Benckiser. NUROFEN, Nurofen target device and Nurofen 'Angel Wings' device are trademarks of the Reckitt Benckiser group of companies

In 1969, ibuprofen was first made available to the public, but it was only available on prescription. In 1983 a branded version, Nurofen, was launched as an OTC (over-the-counter medicine) brand. It was sold with a proposition that said 'a breakthrough in pain relief'. It got to a credible 9 per cent share of its market. However, with a change to the more powerful proposition of 'targeted pain relief' expressed both in new pack graphics – the target (Figure 8.4) – and new advertising it grew rapidly to 27 per cent.[5]

CASE STUDY Tango

Tango is a soft drink primarily sold in the United Kingdom, Ireland, Sweden, Norway, Hungary and Malta, first launched by Corona in 1950. The name Tango came from Ivan Colman saying it had a 'tang'.[6] Corona was bought by the Beecham Group in 1958, and Corona Soft Drinks were bought by Britvic in 1987.

The brand had been promoted with a number of campaigns based around a proposition of 'Made with real oranges'. However, brand performance wasn't great as it was regularly outspent by larger competitors like Fanta, and the proposition and its execution lacked distinctiveness.

In 1991, Tango appointed a new agency, HHCL + Partners, and the proposition changed to 'The hit of real oranges'. This was to be the basis for what was to be a new, highly controversial but hugely successful campaign using the strapline 'You've been Tango'd'. In the first ad of the campaign, the new proposition was translated literally into Tango being personified as an orange man slapping a young man who has just taken a swig of his Tango.[7] Its style was very distinctive, appearing more 'amateur' compared with often very slick, big budget ads of the time.

The ad begins with three young men standing outside a corner shop. One of them takes a sip out of a can of Tango. The voiceover comes from two football-style 'commentators' Ralph and Tony. Ralph says, 'Oh, I think we could use a video replay here,' and the footage of the man drinking the Tango is 'rewound' to before he drinks the Tango, for a 'replay'. This time, a man painted completely orange appears, runs around the men and then taps the Tango drinker on the back.

The Tango drinker turns around, and the orange man slaps him across the cheeks, and then runs off, leaving the drinker startled. Ralph's voiceover becomes excited as he reveals this to be the effect of the 'Tango taste sensation' and asks Tony to rewind the clip again. This time you can see the same action in close up. The advertisement ends with the drinker looking quizzically at his Tango can, followed by a pack shot of the Tango can on top of the orange man's head, which bears the slogan 'You Know When You've Been Tango'd'.

Orange Man made a big impact but was the centre of controversy after reports that children began copying the events of the advertisement in school playgrounds. The first execution was subsequently banned, with another version replacing it in which the orange man kissed the Tango drinker.

Despite the controversy, the ad had a positive impact, leading to a boost of sales by more than a third. It is still widely acclaimed in the industry and features in several lists of the greatest advertisements ever made. A Channel 4/*Sunday Times* poll in 2000 named *Orange Man* the third best advertisement of all time.

The same but different

Examples of how the same proposition can be expressed differently by different brands are shown in Table 8.1.

Table 8.1 Brand propositions

Brand	Proposition
Lufthansa	'There is no better way to fly'
Cascade	'Unbeatable household cleaning'
Gillette	'The best a man can get'

The need to find your brand's own expression of a proposition is further highlighted with the three examples shown in Table 8.1. The actual expressions are all different and yet the proposition at the heart of each of them is the same – nobody does it better.

They are all top-parity claims, where it is true that nobody does it better (including you), so it is currently unbeatable (in comparative tests), and is therefore the best you can get. The claims are distinctive but the proposition isn't differentiated.

Propositions come and go

Propositions don't in general last as long as brand philosophies do. There are exceptions and certain propositions have remained constant for years. Mars' 'helps you work, rest and play', L'Oréal's 'Because you're worth it' and De Beer's 'Diamonds are forever' are classic examples. There are, however, many more that have come and gone or changed or evolved.

If you look at the history of McDonald's advertising taglines in the United Kingdom (which obviously aren't exactly the same as the base proposition) you get a sense of how their proposition has changed over time and how it has varied between a more competitive expression and a more general emotional appeal:

- You'll enjoy the difference (1974)
- There's a difference at McDonald's You'll Enjoy (1974–86)
- It's a Good Time for the Great Taste (1986–88)
- At McDonald's we've got time for you (1985–88)
- A Visit To McDonald's Makes Your Day (1988–92)
- There's nothing quite like a McDonald's (1992–97)
- Enjoy more (1997–2001)
- Only McDonald's (2001–03)
- Things that make you go MMMMMM! (2002–16 September 2003)
- I'm lovin' it (17 September 2003–present)

Comparing this with Germany you can see how the proposition and its expression has obviously changed for different countries and cultural reasons – though it has been aligned since 2003:

- *Das etwas andere Restaurant* (The somewhat different restaurant) (1971–77)
- *Essen mit Spaß* (Eating with fun) (1978–82)
- *Gut, dass es McDonald's gibt* (It's good that McDonald's exists) (1982–87)
- *Der Platz, wo Du gern bist, weil man gut isst* (The place where you like to be because you eat well) (1987–91)
- *McDonald's ist einfach gut* (McDonald's is simply good) (1991–99)
- Every time a good time (1999–1 September 2003)
- *Ich liebe es* (I'm lovin' it) (2 September 2003–present)

However, changing a proposition shouldn't be seen as a problem; rather it's an opportunity to create a more powerful one. The world into which brands are marketed is changing and even the rate of that change is changing – it's accelerating. Expectations change, competitive environments change, new products and services are launched, others reach the end of their life cycles and consequently propositions need to evolve.

This was discussed in Chapter 6 and is a manifestation of Deleuze's definition of something that is constantly changing – and evolving, that has 'porous boundaries' but is still a coherent entity, in his case the analogy of the sand dune, in this case a brand. Modern brands can be likened to an organic entity, constantly growing and changing; new products and services are added, pricing and distribution changes, new propositions come and go. The brand is no longer a static or consistent concept but a coherent idea that adapts how it goes to market to ensure ongoing success.

What makes a good proposition?

To reiterate a proposition is a clear, though not necessarily a single-minded, statement that explains how your product solves a customer's problems or improves their situation by delivering specific benefit(s), and tells that customer why they should buy from you and not from the competition. This could, in fact, be an early definition of a (single product or service) brand but obviously doesn't deliver in the same way for most modern brands.

What then makes for a good proposition? The elements of a good proposition flow naturally from this definition. It should be:

- **clear** and easy to understand;

- **relevant** to the prospective customers' needs (or the needs of the people they are buying it for, whether that's a family or a company);

- **motivating**, promising something(s) that the customer or stake-holder wants and desires. It addresses the customer needs that are either currently unmet or meets them in a way that is more attractive to the customer. It talks to what they want (even if they don't know that they want it yet);

- **distinctive** by being either better, different or cheaper, though as has been discussed, in the modern world where competitors can quickly copy any successful proposition, it may be better to say better, *distinctive* or cheaper. This distinctiveness can be either rationally based – 'washes whiter' – or more emotionally based – 'makes you feel like a good parent' – or indeed it can be both, or just in the way and style in which it is done. As countless blind tests have shown many people can't tell the differences between different products when they aren't overtly branded. In other cases the best performing product isn't always the best-selling one. It has been said that, when it launched, the iPod wasn't the best performing MP3 player but it quickly become the best-selling one;

- **credible**. Returning to a point made earlier, a brand can make any claim but if the people it is addressed to don't believe that the brand can deliver it they are not likely to 'buy' it, and even if they do decide to try it, significantly underperforming is likely to stop any possible repurchase. Overpromising may drive a single sale but over-delivery is actually a better way to build a long-term brand.

Coherent not consistent

As has been discussed the flexibility of this framework is one of the most important differences between it and most other models. It has been designed to incorporate a number of different propositions simultaneously but it is equally important that these are aligned with the overall philosophy. It is this that ensures a coherent set of propositions is developed. Coherent in so far as they are all seen through the lens of the brand philosophy but not completely consistent because they allow for a more nuanced approach to different target groups.

Returning to the original example in this chapter, the central notion of rainbow-ness is the red thread that runs throughout all the different propositions whether they are customers, educational institutions, employees or investors; rainbow-ness provides the core narrative.

A real-world example where the red thread that stems from the core philosophy is very apparent in the whole range of their different propositions is Disney – the core Disney brand rather than the full Disney Corporation, which includes other brands like ABC, Star Wars, Marvel and ESPN.

Again, the specific model shown has been constructed to provide an example for the book so may not be exactly the words they use, or indeed may feel different as I don't believe they use this model. It is, however, based on extensive reading around and about the brand and so I hope feels instinctively true.

CASE STUDY Disney

Disney's purpose is around creating a magical world of family entertainment, which makes people happy. Central to this is the notion and belief in storytelling as a wonderful media. It is a purpose that has allowed the brand to stretch way beyond its origins in animated films into products, retail outlets, TV channels, websites, games, theme parks and cruises to mention just a few parts of what is undoubtedly one of the world's biggest and most powerful brands (Figure 8.5).

It does, however, have limits in its dedication to family entertainment; being suitable for all the family means it does say 'No' to certain ideas. *Pretty Woman*

Figure 8.5 Example of how Disney could be expressed in the new brand framework

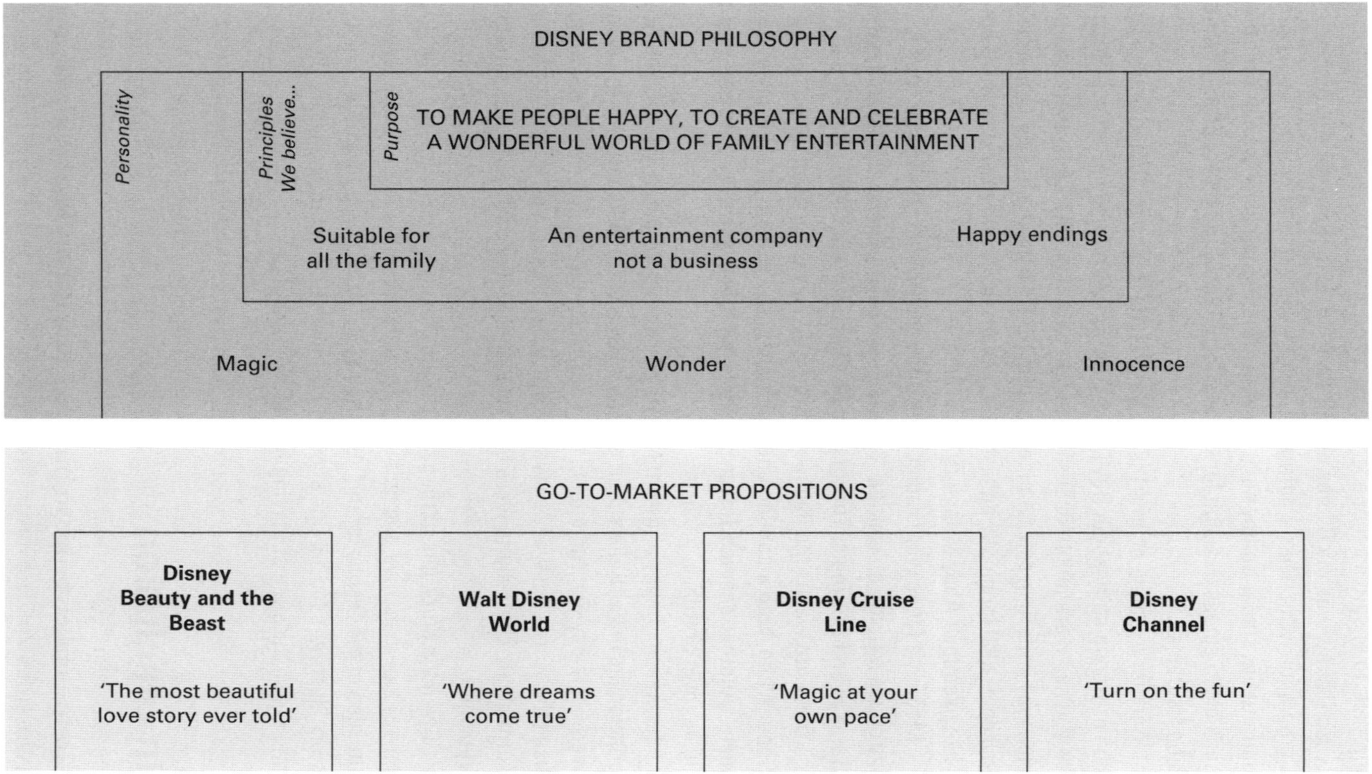

DISNEY BRAND PHILOSOPHY

Personality		
Principles We believe...	Suitable for all the family	An entertainment company not a business	Happy endings
Purpose	TO MAKE PEOPLE HAPPY, TO CREATE AND CELEBRATE A WONDERFUL WORLD OF FAMILY ENTERTAINMENT		

Magic   Wonder   Innocence

GO-TO-MARKET PROPOSITIONS

Disney Beauty and the Beast	**Walt Disney World**	**Disney Cruise Line**	**Disney Channel**
'The most beautiful love story ever told'	'Where dreams come true'	'Magic at your own pace'	'Turn on the fun'

was a great script, Disney is a great film maker with the distribution and marketing skills to ensure its success. It wasn't and isn't a Disney film though.

So Disney, well the Disney brand, said 'No' to it. However, the Disney Corporation, which has a different purpose and set of principles, could see the opportunity. Under another of its brands, Touchstone films, it said 'Yes'. A very sensible business decision for Disney Corporation and a very proper brand decision for Disney.

Another example of how Disney has stayed true to the brand and its principles comes from a story about Roy Disney, Tinker Bell and some T-shirts. Back in 2000, times were tough for Disney and, in particular, the Consumer Products division was suffering; sales had fallen from US \$900 million in 1997 to just US \$386 million in 2000 (originally published in *The Prisoner and the Penguin*).[8] Former Nike executive Andy Mooney was hired to try to rejuvenate the business.

Mooney's ideas were radical – at times very radical. It was his idea to introduce a range of 'vintage' T-shirts in upscale clothing shops like Fred Segal, Barneys and Hot Topic. The images on the shirts were taken from the archives.

The issue wasn't the images but the way they were used. One T-shirt showed Snow White, with a caption underneath saying, 'Hangs out with seven small men'.[9] Another showed Tinker Bell in a shot that made it look like she was eyeing up her own bottom in a mirror.

Roy wasn't happy and sent Mooney a handwritten note, which said: 'You are positioning Tinker Bell as a prostitute.'[10] For a brand dedicated to 'the wonderful world of family entertainment', this was a step too far. Roy would never have used the words but what he was saying was: 'Stop it, you're way off-brand'. Not surprisingly, the T-shirts were quickly withdrawn and Mooney was forced to apologize.

Given the story, it is perhaps a little surprising to learn that Roy Disney, a long-time senior executive and nephew of founder Walt Disney, actually never liked the idea of the Disney 'brand'. He once said, 'Branding is for cattle', but as the story illustrates his actions showed his innate understanding of the Disney brand and the importance of staying true to its principles.

In conclusion

Go-to-market propositions and brand philosophy are akin to the two sides on the same coin. They are related and complementary. Propositions should be rooted in, and coherent with the purpose and principles of the brand but need to be based on customer understanding to ensure that they are relevant, credible, clear, distinctive and, most importantly, motivating.

While there is only one philosophy, there should be multiple propositions. They are the promises the brand makes, which need to be specific to the different stakeholder and target groups and they are action orientated.

However, unlike the core brand philosophy they may well be shorter term as markets, competitors and customers' needs, tastes and expectations change, and so how the brand expresses that promise or indeed innovates with new products and services needs to change too.

Getting the propositions right can mean the difference between success and failure. A brand with a well-defined philosophy can still fail if it doesn't have good go-to-market propositions.

Propositions compromise four or five key elements: the frame of reference, the target audience, insights about that group, the benefits and the reasons to believe.

The propositions can be rationally or emotionally based and, in fact, most often are a combination of the two, but with the proportion of 'emo' and 'func' varying (Figure 8.6).

A functionally-led proposition might be 'Kills 99% of known germs. Dead.' while a more emotionally led proposition might be I ♥ NY.

Again, it is often assumed that a proposition needs to be single-minded but many, especially B2B propositions, are often multifaceted.

Figure 8.6 Different propositions can have different weighting of emotional and functional elements

SOURCE The Value Engineers (2017)

Notes

1 Seminars on Demand (2008) [accessed 18 January 2017] *The Power of Vision* [Video] 4 November 2008 [Online] https://www.youtube.com/watch?v=aYsS2bIPXio

2 Arkwright, D (2014) [accessed 18 January 2017] Dirt is Good: How storytelling gave Persil a boost, *Campaign* [Online] http://www.campaignlive.co.uk/article/1287039/dirt-good-storytelling-gave-persil-boost#GmGSE6vIXmmLbuRX.99

3 Kantar Vermeer (2017) [accessed 18 January 2017] *OMO: Unlocking Global Brand Potential* [Online] http://mbvermeer.com/omo-unlocking-global-brand-potential/

4 Talking Retail (2017) [accessed 10 March 2017] 'I Can't Believe It's Not Butter' Gets a Re-brand [Online] http://www.talkingretail.com/products-news/chilled/cant-believe-butter-gets-re-brand/

5 Brades, J (1990) *Nurofen: Turning Heads in the Analgesic Market*, Institute of Practitioners in Advertising, IPA Effectiveness Awards

6 Youthrank (no date) [accessed 7 February 2017] *Digital Benchmarking for the Youth Sector* [Online] https://www.youthrank.com/brand/tango

7 Marcel Visser (2007) [accessed: 18 January 2017] Tango Commercial – *Orange Man* [Online Video] 27 October 2007 [Online] https://www.youtube.com/watch?v=ZfE2RSdemlQ

8 Lury, G (2013) *The Prisoner and the Penguin*, 1st edn, LID Publishing, London

9 *The Scotsman* (2005) [accessed 7 February 2017] Roy disnae agree with mickey taking [Online] http://www.scotsman.com/business/management/roy-disnae-agree-with-mickey-taking-1-1389011

10 *The Scotsman* (2005) [accessed 7 February 2017] Roy disnae agree with mickey taking [Online] http://www.scotsman.com/business/management/roy-disnae-agree-with-mickey-taking-1-1389011

A new marketing 09 mindset

'It's all in the mind, you know?'
GEORGE HARRISON IN *YELLOW SUBMARINE* 1968

Old habits die hard

While it may seem that much of this book has been the background and build-up to the new Marketing Complex Framework introduced in the previous chapters, it is in fact as much about the need for a change in mindset. The framework is just a means of setting out the thinking; people may yet find new shapes and forms for it or variations of it for themselves. This isn't a problem and is something to be welcomed as it would represent that the thinking is being accepted and built upon.

It is this thinking that is probably the most important aspect of the book. It challenges some long-held assumptions and deep-rooted behaviours. The book is really a call for a new marketing mindset. It asks people to think differently and to act differently.

Talking to a colleague who has been working with the framework with a number of his clients, he described what he said was something that happened to him with surprising regularity:

> 'Initially clients buy into the thinking and into the framework. They can see its benefits. It gives them an approach, which immediately and intuitively makes sense. They say they get it, but at some point they or someone in their team will almost inevitably say, "Come on, let's cut to the chase; what's the one thing that really differentiates us?" It's then that you realize old habits die hard. You understand how long it takes to change the habits of a lifetime.'

The siren call of simplification is still strong. The urge to look for a single consumer or customer-focused differentiating proposition remains, even if most marketers would say they know the fallacy of the USP.

Many have been taught at university, business school and/or in their jobs about how single-mindedness is good and multiplicity is bad. Their agencies, whether they are advertising or design and to a lesser extent digital agencies, have all reinforced the desirability of singularity. Ries and Trout's book is still on most must-read book lists and even if people don't read the whole book they hear the 'over-communicated–oversimplified' soundbite time and time again.

This 'simplicity is good and complexity is bad' thinking is itself a reflection of oversimplification. It is an example of what Edward De Bono and others have called 'binary thinking'.

In *I Am Right, You Are Wrong* by Dr Edward de Bono (2009), he argues against many of the assumptions inherent in classical thought, including the notion of universally accepted objective truth and the binary structures that are foundational to logic (winner/loser, right/wrong, true/false) and which posit argument as adversarial.[1]

Binary thinking reduces all arguments to a simple two-way choice between something that is right and something that is wrong. De Bono highlights how this oversimplified approach is prevalent in huge swathes of contemporary and social discourse: in formal situations like courtrooms and legislative bodies, in the pages of scientific journals and in the op-ed sections of newspapers the world over. Equally, it can be seen in much of the thinking about good parenting and in our educational systems.[2]

In school, we are taught there are right and wrong answers: 2 + 2 = 4 not 5, not 4.5. If left was right then right was wrong. It's black or white. Unfortunately, in the world generally and in marketing specifically the reality is that it is shades of grey and all of the wonderful colours under the sun too!

In science, discovery is built on the premise of exploring a single hypothesis that you test and test, and if it still holds after all that then it becomes a 'law' – that is until someone breaks it! In economics you learn the rule of 'ceteris paribus' or 'all other things being equal', which is great and makes modelling so much easier until you realize all those other things never remain equal.

The writer Faris Yakob, author of *Paid Attention*, suggests that:

'we always look for the super simple "insight" even in areas that are amazingly complex, like cognitive research. We are biased towards simplicity because we only ever encounter complexity in the real world.

Hence, stories and myths and how memory works and the oft spouted belief in simplicity, which often masks or distorts instead of reflecting reality.'[3]

It's time marketers understood that for lots of questions in the real world there is no one right answer, there are lots of right answers. Branding isn't a science – it's messy, constantly changing, it's ambiguous. Many marketers like rules and laws, even immutable ones; they provide order, structure and predictability. They make life easier. Unfortunately, in branding there just aren't any. For every branding law there are exceptions; for every rule there are brands who successfully break them.

CASE STUDY Take two car brands, Porsche and Toyota

When, in 2002, Porsche wanted to move out of producing just sports cars they did so by extending their existing brand name and launching a new model, the Cayenne, into the SUV sector. At the time it was seen as a controversial move, as some customers and motoring journalists felt the maker of the 911 shouldn't be launching a car more likely to be seen dropping off kids at school than on a race track. However, thanks to bringing great performance to the sector, retaining the Porsche styling ethos, the Cayenne was a major success story. In the United Kingdom, it helped fuel 'growth of 60% over 3 years. Globally, the Cayenne made up 50% of Porsche's volume'.[4]

When Toyota wanted to extend into luxury cars internationally, they created a completely new brand – Lexus. Lexus originated from a corporate project, code-named F1. Toyota had struggled to take its brand into the luxury sector outside of its home country but desperately wanted to gain a foothold in this prestigious and profitable sector. The project began in 1983 and culminated in the launch of the Lexus LS in 1989. Subsequently, the new brand added sedan, coupé, convertible and SUV models. It was not until 2005 that it was launched in Japan. In its home market, all vehicles marketed internationally as Lexus from 1989 to 2005 were released in Japan under the Toyota brand with an equivalent model name. In 2005, a hybrid version of the RX crossover debuted in Japan, and additional hybrid models later joined the division's line-up. It has become Japan's largest-selling make of premium cars.

Two different approaches, two very successful answers to the same question.

Are you addicted to oversimplification?

Psychology Today (2017) defines addiction as:

> 'a condition that results when a person ingests a substance (eg, alcohol, cocaine, nicotine) or engages in an activity (eg, gambling, sex, shopping) that can be pleasurable but the continued use/act of which becomes compulsive and interferes with ordinary life responsibilities, such as work, relationships, or health. Users may not be aware that their behavior is out of control and causing problems for themselves and others.'[5]

Based on which, but perhaps to a lesser degree, it doesn't seem unreasonable to suggest that marketers' fixation on single-mindedness is an addiction. Marketers have become addicted to oversimplification. It has become a compulsion for many marketers, to the extent that they perhaps subconsciously ignore exceptions that don't fit the rule.

Used responsibly, simplification can be very valuable. It makes their life easier. It is easy to understand, easy to communicate. It provides clarity but it is not always the right answer. Moderate usage of alcohol or shopping has benefits but isn't and shouldn't be the be all and end all.

Sometimes things just aren't simple. They can't be reduced to a single causality or indeed to a single benefit. Quantum physics isn't simple nor is human behaviour, which in turn is one of the reasons why marketing isn't a pure science. At best, it is a social science. My colleague Paul Walton describes it as a mixture of a 'bastard science and a black art'.

The drive for simplification and, as we have seen, its extreme expression as singularity, however, has become ingrained. It is taught in business schools, universities and companies' own marketing training schemes throughout the world. It has been built into marketing processes and templates. Behaviours that fit the model are encouraged and rewarded. Contradicting it is wrong, accepting it is right.

As mentioned earlier most propositions, even if expressed as a single sentence, are often a summary of a number of benefits.

CASE STUDY Ronseal – it does what it says on the tin

HHCL & Partners was the hot agency of the 1990s. The partners appeared on the front cover of the prestigious *Sunday Times Magazine*. It was the first advertising agency to stop calling itself an advertising agency, and rename itself a communications agency. They were voted 'Agency of the Decade' by *Campaign* magazine in 2000,[6] but after a series of mergers and a name change to United London, the agency was closed in early 2007. It created a number of impactful, and often controversial, campaigns, the proposition for which has become part of the marketing world's vernacular: 'doing a Ronseal' – to do what it says on the tin.[7]

From a conversation we had back in 2012, Adam Lury, one of the founding partners and planning director recalls:

'We sent several classic 'clever' HHCL ads out to test with the target audience who were predominantly male DIYers and matter-of-fact men who took a "no nonsense" approach to life.

'The planner, Ruth Lees, came back to me after the research a bit shell-shocked and said: "This target audience didn't like them. In fact, they were proudly boasting that they didn't just not like these ads, they hated all advertising. They wanted nothing to do with any idea."

'So I said to her, "Well don't advertise to them then".

'She took that thought back to the project team, and from that built the idea of the non-advertising advertising.'

So instead of trying to sell to them, Ruth and the team came up with the idea of just telling them what the product did in a no-nonsense way and 'Ronseal – it does exactly what it says on the tin' was born.

On one level, this is a single-minded proposition – but is it really?

Is the benefit that Ronseal products are highly effective and so get the job done?

Or is it the benefit that, here is a brand that doesn't try to fool you with 'clever advertising' so you can really trust it? (And in doing so, you actually fall for the double-bluff in the line – it is very clever advertising that is seducing you into buying it.)

Or is the benefit that, here is a no-nonsense brand that is the brand for me, a no-nonsense sort of person?

It is the beauty and, I believe, its strength that it isn't any one of them: it is all of them.

The first step is to recognize the problem

It was traditionally said that it took 21 days repeatedly doing something for it to become a habit. Recent research by University College London suggests it might actually be longer. Their research indicated that it takes an average of 66 days to create a habit.[8] The drive for single-mindedness in marketing has probably had 66 years!

So how will marketers break this habit of a lifetime and cure their addiction to oversimplification? Addiction theory would suggest it starts with genuinely admitting that there is a problem in the first place, and currently not enough marketers believe that there is one.

CASE STUDY

In the very first episode of the HBO television series *The Newsroom* there is a scene on a university campus. A panel including news anchor Will McAvoy, played by Jeff Daniels, is asked to say what makes the United States the greatest country in the world – in one sentence (the classic demand for a simplistic soundbite again).

His fellow panellists reply with pat responses 'Diversity and opportunity' and 'Freedom and freedom'.

His first response is a somewhat glib 'The New York Jets'. Pushed by the host to truly answer the question, he replies that America is no longer the greatest country in the world and gives a whole string of reasons about how other countries have caught up and overtaken it on a number of measures. He says America may have been able to claim it in the past but it can't any more.

Then, towards the end of his impassioned speech, he looks to the future and says: 'The first step in solving any problem is recognizing there is one.'[9]

You can watch the clip here: https://www.youtube.com/watch?v=wTjMqda19wk

It a very powerful 3 minutes and 30 seconds, well worth a watch and it not only emphasizes the need to admit the problem but mirrors a number of other themes in this book and a number of points about the changes required to the marketers' mindset.

It starts with a demand for an oversimplified answer.

The answers given are, to the audience at least at first, reasonable and appealing. Later though, with a little honest challenge, they can be shown quite quickly not only to be simplistic but wrong. The real answer is much more complicated and involves a number of themes and ideas. And, of course, McAvoy points out that the suggested first step to finding a better answer is to admit honestly that there is a problem.

Not pure and never simple

An earlier but equally apt quote comes from Oscar Wilde who, in his 1895 play *The Importance of Being Earnest* wrote: 'The pure and simple truth is rarely pure and never simple'.[10]

Also from around the turn of the 20th century is the Einstein quote, which is perhaps one of the most important ideas in this book: 'Everything should be made as simple as possible… but not any simpler'. This quote, generally attributed to Einstein, is thought to come from a letter written by him and sent to Jost Winteler (1901). There is, however, some debate as to whether he did ever actually say or write that exact phrase.

However, there is no debate that he did say and then write:

'It can scarcely be denied that the supreme goal of all theory is to make the irreducible basic elements as simple and as few as possible without having to surrender the adequate representation of a single datum of experience.'[11]

Interestingly, the discussion around this longer quote is often linked to the notion of Occam's razor. This is the principle, attributed to William of Occam, arguing that in explaining something, no more assumptions should be made than are necessary. It advocates that among all hypotheses compatible with all available observations, the simplest hypothesis is the most plausible one. The principle is, not surprisingly, invoked to defend reductionism or nominalism.

What is interesting is that too often it is reduced to the idea that the simplest assumptions are the best. For example, Wikipedia, a source that perhaps also suffers from oversimplification at times, states: 'Occam's razor (or Ockham's razor) is a principle from philosophy. Suppose there exist two explanations for an occurrence. In this case, the simpler one is usually better'.[12]

These oversimplifications can miss out the important phrases 'compatible with all available observations', 'than are necessary' and Einstein's original 'without having to surrender the adequate representation of a single datum of experience'. Too often in marketing, the notion is that 'Everything should be made as simple as possible' and the all-important four qualifying words 'but not any simpler' are ignored or conveniently forgotten.

The old mindset

The attributes needed to become a successful marketer are many and varied. Traditionally, the following 5Cs – collaborative, customer-centric, commercial, clever and (good) communicators – are all often mentioned:

1 **Collaborative** – many marketers like to think they sit at the heart of their organization, but then so do many other people in many other departments or functions.

It is probably truer to say marketing is closely interlinked with many other departments within the organization including sales, production, supply chain, R&D, corporate affairs, HR and finance. In addition, they will normally work with a range of external agencies and consultancies including PR, design, digital, research and advertising agencies. With all of them, they need to work productively and constructively so a collaborative approach and mentality is required to get the most out of themselves and their partners. Marketers need to recognize that their success relies on their co-dependency and cooperation with others.

As recruitment brand Monster puts it:

'The job requires a lot of skill and the ability to manage people from a range of different disciplines. One minute you may be dealing with a team of marketing executives the next you could be liaising with the people in PR, production, merchandising, manufacturing, sales, distribution or finance. So you need to understand how each role within the organisation operates and be able to bring together these varying skills sets and direct them accordingly.'[13]

2 Customer-centric – if the customer is king in the world of marketing then being customer-centric is a no-brainer. As we have seen, marketing is sometimes defined as 'satisfying customers' needs profitably' so being interested in people, what motivates and drives them is a prerequisite. Customer-centricity, while increasingly seen as important for many parts of any business – especially in service businesses, is seen as the core remit of marketers and Consumer, Marketing and Intelligence (CMI) departments.

Customer-centricity is complemented by other forms of 'centricity', which can be the basis for other forms of marketing strategy but which are often seen as being as much the remit of other business specialisms as they are of marketing. Product-centricity (competitive advantage through superior product design) is linked to R&D and production. Channel-centricity (focus on achieving dominance in one or more channels) is linked with sales and trade marketing.

3 Commercial – having highlighted the first half of the definition of marketing and its focus on customers' needs, the second half of that definition – 'profitably' – is equally important. Most brands must make profits to be sustainable, and even marketers running not-for-profit brands must be commercially astute. Efficient and effective use of time, resources and budget are key to being a good marketer.

It has been said that the lack of real commercial acumen and the failure to prove marketing ROIs are two of the barriers that have meant many CMOs never become CEOs. A talent for the commercial side of things is therefore something not always found in marketers, but highly prized when it is.

As Philip Kotler, Kellogg School of Management, Northwestern University, wrote in his article 'Marketing: The unappreciated workhorse': 'Marketers need to improve their metrics and measurement of the financial impact of their marketing activities and campaigns. Senior management is losing patience with marketing over the lack of marketing results measurement'.[14]

Many marketers will try to make a case for more budget at every opportunity, but perhaps a better test of a good marketer is to ask them what they could achieve if they had only half the budget. As the scientist, Ernest Rutherford said, when considering how to compete against the better-funded scientists of the United States: 'We've got no money, so we've got to think'.[15]

4 **Clever** – good marketers need to be intelligent. Traditionally, and indeed currently, many people say they need to be 'centre-brain thinkers' (Figure 9.1): 'Generally it is felt that some people are left brained and some are right brained. Left brained are analytical in their approach and right brained are creative, artistic. A marketer needs to be both brained to bring discipline as well as art to the profession'.[16]

Figure 9.1 Attributes associated with left- and right-brain thinking

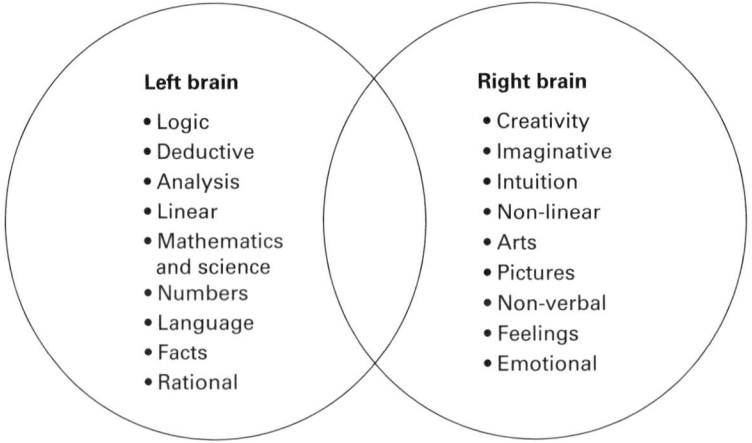

Left brain	Right brain
• Logic	• Creativity
• Deductive	• Imaginative
• Analysis	• Intuition
• Linear	• Non-linear
• Mathematics and science	• Arts
• Numbers	• Pictures
• Language	• Non-verbal
• Facts	• Feelings
• Rational	• Emotional

Now, if marketers are really clever they will actually know that the whole notion of left- and right-brain thinking has been discredited. As Amy Novotney wrote in *The Guardian* in 2013:

'The theory that the different halves of the human brain govern different skills and personality traits is a popular one. No doubt at some point in your life you've been schooled on "left-brained" and "right-brained" thinking.

Too bad it's not true.'[17]

Studies, including those by University of Utah, have shown that the facts don't support the notion and that, in fact, it is another case of oversimplification.

'The neuroscience community has never accepted the idea of "left-dominant" or "right-dominant" personality types. Lesion studies don't support it, and the truth is that it would be highly inefficient for one half of the brain to consistently be more active than the other.'

Jeff Anderson, professor of neuroradiology
at the University of Utah (2013)[18]

The truth is far more complex. Brain function is more complicated and the attributes attributed to the left or the right are to some extent dependent on functions in the other side of the brain but, as Novotney (2013) predicted, this truth hasn't got in the way of a good story and the terms haven't disappeared from general usage. The seductively simple labelling of analytical left-brain and creative right-brain thinking is still widely quoted.

5 **Communicators** – while there are clear differences between sales and marketing, and sales people and marketers, a marketer still needs to be able to sell an idea. Like the best lawyers, marketers have to be able to build and deliver persuasive arguments. Internally or externally, marketers need to be good advocates.

Communicating and connecting with people from within and beyond the business is a key skill for the successful marketer.

A final C might sum up the role of a good marketing manager and that is a **Conductor**: 'Just like the conductor who controls the orchestra, [marketing] managers are responsible for ensuring that every single member of their team – regardless of whether you are managing a team of 2 or 200 people – is working in cohesion with each other towards achieving the same outcome'.[19]

So, like any conductor, a marketing manager aims to pull everything together, create something that is beautifully harmonious and avoid creating a discordant cacophony.

The new mindset

The new mindset doesn't mean that all these attributes – the 5Cs – will no longer be required but it does call for marketers to rethink their own approach and expectations.

Break out of binary thinking

The notion of one singular right answer or solution is something that has been ingrained into much of what marketers do and the theory behind it; they will need to challenge themselves and others to break out from the search for singularity. Marketers may (claim to) no longer talk about the Unique Selling Proposition, but there is still the core target audience, *the* killer insight; *the*-single-thing-you-most-want-to-communicate and, of course, *the* 'big idea'. There is a trend towards single-figure scores, and a notion that *the only* way to do innovation is to be consumer-led.

There are just too many definite articles. Marketers will need to engage their brains more and all their skills as communicators to advocate a new approach that might, at first, sound like heresy to the accepted dogma of traditional marketing.

A tool used by my colleagues at The Value Engineers to help people think differently is this simple 'odd one out' test (Figure 9.2):

Ask a group of people and you are likely to get some answers along the lines of:

- 'It's B because it's the only one with all straight edges.'
- 'It's D because it's the only one with two bits taken out of it.'
- 'It's C because it's the only one with a dotted effect.'

Figure 9.2   The 'No One Right Answer' test

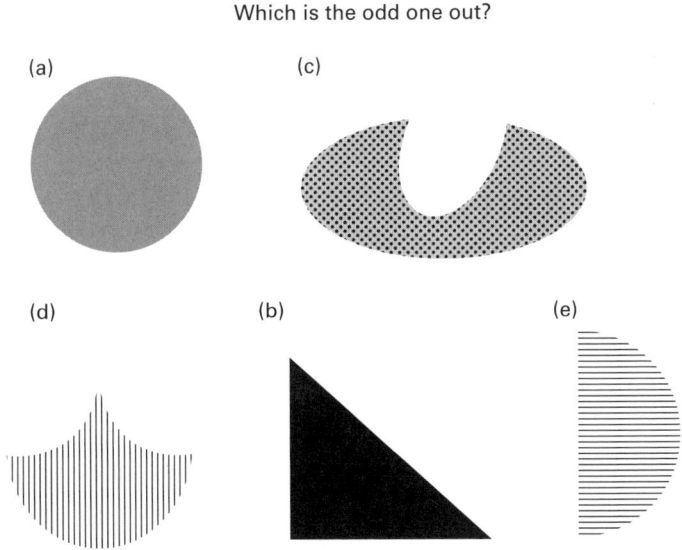

SOURCE The Value Engineers (2017)

Of course, all the answers are correct and, in fact, a case can success-fully be made for each of these shapes to be the odd one out. It's a quick way to get people to realize that there is often more than one right answer.

Look deeper and challenge more

Too many marketing 'laws' aren't laws. As discussed earlier, the underlying premise of an oversimplified message working better and consumers' ability to take out only one thing from a message has no real scientific basis and there are numerous examples of where this is patently just not true. It is the marketing equivalent of the old hypothesis that Earth was at the centre of the universe and the sun rotated around it.

Too often supported by just a few well-loved brand examples, what at best is a generalization is accepted as a 'law'. Sometimes, it seems that in marketing if one's an incidence, two's a coincidence, and three must be a law.

Marketers need to challenge themselves and others more. What is happening is what was discussed earlier in this chapter, namely that the law of oversimplifications ignores the fact that there is not compatibility with 'all available observations'.

The same is true of other marketing thinking and it's time to take a leaf out of the title of Robert Kriegel and David Brandt's famous book and realize that *Sacred Cows Make the Best Burgers*.[20]

Don't expect it to be easy

An oversimplified message in an over-communicated world, which probably qualifies as an overused quote in this book, suggests an easy solution. It is easy to communicate, easy to manage, easy to persuade people that it is right. In a chaotic world, it suggests a comfortable way forward.

It is an illusion. Managing a brand is not easy. The reality is that today's brands operate in a chaotic world. They need to cross boundaries of category, country and audience. They have to engage different stakeholder groups with different messages and experiences at different times and in different places – all while maintaining a coherent, though not necessarily an absolutely consistent brand attitude.

Modern brands need depth and variety. Managing those brands is complex and difficult.

I would suggest that some of the ideas and concepts in this book aren't simple. For example, I haven't argued against simplification per se or its benefits, but I have argued against oversimplification. If something can be simplified to a single-minded proposition, which does all it's needed to do, then that's great. However, what I have suggested is that in many if not most cases things can be simplified to a certain extent but no more. It's not as clean, it's not as easy but few things in life are clean and easy. If marketing were easy then it probably wouldn't be as enjoyable and challenging as it is, and I probably would be out of a job, and so might you.

(Get on your bike and) Embrace multiplicity

In 2010, Dave Brailsford became the new General Manager and Performance Director for Team Sky (Great Britain's professional cycling team) and was set the unenviable task of ensuring that a British cyclist won the Tour de France: something that had never happened in the 100+ years the race had been run. Brailsford believed that if all went to plan, Team Sky could be in a position to win the Tour de France within five years. They actually won it just three years later.

How did Brailsford and his team achieve it? What was the one single thing that made the difference? The answer, of course, was that it wasn't one single thing that made all the difference but a whole series of things.

Brailsford believed in what is an example of multiplicity in action. He set out not to change one thing but to look for improvements in everything, an approach that he called the 'aggregation of marginal gains.' He and his team would search for 'the 1 per cent margin for improvement in everything you do'. His belief was that if you improved every area related to cycling by just 1 per cent, then those small gains would add up to remarkable improvement.

They started on what were perhaps the more obvious aspects of performance: the nutrition of riders, their weekly training programme, the ergonomics of the bike seat and the weight of the tyres.

This was, however, just the beginning. Brailsford and his team went in search of those 1 per cent improvements in even the smallest areas which weren't so obvious and which were overlooked by most other teams. They found the pillow that helped the riders get the best night's sleep and took it with them to hotels. They tested numerous massage gels before choosing the one that was effective. They even taught their riders the best way to wash their hands to avoid infection. Multiple little improvements and then, in 2012, Team Sky rider Sir Bradley Wiggins became the first British cyclist to win the Tour de France.

CASE STUDY Premier Inn

A parallel brand example might be Premier Inn. A quick look at their website and you can see that they have embraced marketing multiplicity:

'Why we're Premier

Is it our beds, our food, our great value or our people that people love so much? Perhaps it's a bit of everything. Anyway, take a look around to find out why we keep winning all these lovely awards.'[21]

And the parallel goes further: Premier Inn seem to have gone looking for those marginal gains in all they offer. One strand of their offer is based on their belief that great days start with a good night's sleep, so not surprisingly: 'We've thought of everything you need to have a great night's sleep so you wake up ready to take on the world.'[22]

What this means in practice is:

- a good night guarantee – they're so confident that you'll have a great night's sleep that, if you don't, they'll give you your money back;

- the best ever bed or as they say 'At Premier Inn, you're not just getting out of the right side of the bed – you're getting out of the right bed! In every one of our Premier Inn hotels, you'll find a luxury kingsize Hypnos bed, guaranteed to send you off to a great night's sleep. With a thousand pocket springs supporting a pillow-top mattress, a toasty duvet and your choice of pillows, our bed is the stuff of dreams'.[23]

Then, if you have had a wonderful night's sleep you might want to take the bed home with you. You can't actually take the bed from your room home with you but you can do the next best thing as Premier Inn have teamed up with Hypnos and you can buy your very own Hypnos bed and have it delivered to your home:

- The right pillow – they offer not just a choice of pillow but advice on which is likely to be best for you, depending on whether you sleep on your back, your side or your front.

- Free audiobooks to help you 'drift away'.

- 'Sleep tips' for little dreamers – top sleep tips to help kids nod off in no time.

Premier Inn are winners too: not of the 'Tour de Dormir', but they are the UK's top-rated hotel chain.[24]

Nine out of ten Premier Inn hotels received TripAdvisor's Certificate of Excellence in 2016 – that amounted to 621 of their hotels across the United Kingdom.[25] They are number 1 in TripAdvisor's Best Family Hotels in the UK.[26] They were named the UK's top-rated hotel chain in the *Which? Hotel* report 2015.[27]

Their ability to manage and deliver the necessary multiplicity of a great night's sleep has led to a multiplicity of awards.

Start a revolution (when branding)

I started this section by saying that the 5Cs remain valid and that the new mindset doesn't mean that those attributes will no longer be required. To finish this chapter I want to both endorse and to some extent challenge it or at least challenge one of the Cs.

As argued in earlier chapters when it comes to marketing, the customer is still king and so customer-centricity, of course, remains key for marketers.

When it comes to branding, the best brands come from within and the customer is just one stakeholder and may not even be the most important one. When it comes to defining your brand's philosophy and principles, an important role for any marketer, it's time to start a revolution and dethrone the customer. So until the roles of marketing and branding are completely separated, marketers will have to accept the ambiguity of customers as part-time royalty.

So, in keeping with the notion of no one right answer and the need to embrace multiplicity and ambiguity, I will finish with a quote from F Scott Fitzgerald (1936): 'The test of a first-rate intelligence is the ability to hold two opposing ideas in mind at the same time and still retain the ability to function'.[28]

Notes

1   De Bono, E (2009) *I Am right, You Are Wrong*, 1st edn, Viking, London

2   De Bono, E (2009) *I Am right, You Are Wrong*, 1st edn, Viking, London

3   Yakob, F (2015) [accessed 10 March 2017] The Axes of Attention, *LinkedIn* [Online] https://www.linkedin.com/pulse/axes-attention-faris-yakob?trk=hp-feed-article-title-like

4   The Porsche Cayenne: Successful stretch (2011) [accessed 6 February 2017] [Blog] *The brandgym blog* [Online] http://wheresthesausage.typepad.com/my_weblog/2011/11/the-porsche-cayenne-successful-stretch-.html

5   Addiction: Substance abuse (2017) [accessed 6 February 2017] *Psychology Today* [Online] https://www.psychologytoday.com/basics/addiction

6   Wnek, M (2000) [accessed 10 March 2017] Agency of the Decade: HHCL & Partners – HHCL proved its mettle with a canny combination of business initiatives and daring creative work such as Tango, setting the pace for advertising in the 90s, *Campaign* [Online] http://www.campaignlive.co.uk/article/agency-decade-hhcl-partners-hhcl-proved-its-mettle-canny-combination-business-initiatives-daring-creative-work-tango-setting-pace-advertising-90s/35096

7 Wnek, M (2000) [accessed 10 March 2017] Agency of the Decade: HHCL & Partners – HHCL proved its mettle with a canny combination of business initiatives and daring creative work such as Tango, setting the pace for advertising in the 90s, *Campaign* [Online] http://www.campaignlive.co.uk/article/agency-decade-hhcl-partners-hhcl-proved-its-mettle-canny-combination-business-initiatives-daring-creative-work-tango-setting-pace-advertising-90s/35096

8 Gardener, B and Meisel, S (2012) [accessed 6 February 2017] Busting the 21 days habit formation myth, *UCL 'Health Chatter': The Health Behaviour Research Centre Blog* [Online] http://blogs.ucl.ac.uk/hbrc/2012/06/29/busting-the-21-days-habit-formation-myth/

9 tpratt441 (21 July 2012) [accessed: 6 February 2017] *The Newsroom* – America is not the greatest country in the world anymore [Online Video] https://www.youtube.com/watch?v=wTjMqda19wk

10 Wilde, O (1990) *The Importance of Being Earnest*, 1st edn, Dover Publications, New York

11 Einstein, A (1934) On the Method of Theoretical Physics, *Philosophy of Science*, **1** (2), pp 163–9, Retrieved from http://www.jstor.org/stable/184387

12 Wikipedia (2017) [accessed 6 February 2017] Occam's razor [Online] https://simple.wikipedia.org/wiki/Occam's_razor

13 Monster Career Advice (no date) [accessed 6 February 2017] What attributes make a good Marketing manager? [Online] https://www.monster.co.uk/career-advice/article/what-attributes-make-a-good-marketing-manager

14 Kotler, P (2009) [accessed 10 March 2017] *Market Leader: 50 years of The Marketing Society*, The Marketing Society [Online] https://www.marketingsociety.com/sites/default/files/thelibrary/march-2009_10.pdf

15 Andrade, E (1964) *Rutherford and the Nature of the Atom*, 1st edn, Doubleday, Garden City, NY

16 Ravani, S (2015) [accessed 6 February 2017] Top 14 Skills and Qualities of a Successful Marketing Executive, *WiseStep* [Online] http://content.wisestep.com/top-skills-and-qualities-of-a-successful-marketing-executive/

17 Novotney, A (2013) [accessed 6 February 2017] Despite what you've been told, you aren't 'left-brained' or 'right-brained', *The Guardian* [Online] https://www.theguardian.com/commentisfree/2013/nov/16/left-right-brain-distinction-myth

18 Nielsen, J A, Zielinski, B A, Ferguson, M A, Lainhart, J E and Anderson, J S (2013) An Evaluation of the Left-Brain vs. Right-Brain Hypothesis with Resting State Functional Connectivity Magnetic Resonance Imaging, *PLoS ONE* 8 (8): e71275. doi:10.1371/journal.pone.0071275

19 Monster Career Advice (no date) [accessed 30 March 2017] What attributes make a good Marketing manager? [Online] https://www.monster.co.uk/career-advice/article/what-attributes-make-a-good-marketing-manager

20 Kriegel, R and Brandt, D (2011) *Sacred Cows Make the Best Burgers*, 1st edn, Business Plus, New York

21 Premier Inn (2017) [accessed 6 February 2017] Why we're Premier [Online] http://www.premierinn.com/gb/en/why.html

22 Premier Inn (2017) [accessed 6 February 2017] Why we're Premier [Online] http://www.premierinn.com/gb/en/why.html

23 Lury, G (2016) [accessed 6 February 2017] And so to bed…: What we can all learn about managing customer experience from Premier Inn, *The Marketing Society* [Online] https://www.marketingsociety.com/the-gym/and-so-bed%E2%80%A6#2HaSUa1ZCZr6VCgR.99

24 Lury, G (2016) [accessed 6 February 2017] And so to bed…: What we can all learn about managing customer experience from Premier Inn, *The Marketing Society* [Online] https://www.marketingsociety.com/the-gym/and-so-bed%E2%80%A6#2HaSUa1ZCZr6VCgR.99

25 Lury, G (2016) [accessed 6 February 2017] And so to bed…: What we can all learn about managing customer experience from Premier Inn, *The Marketing Society* [Online] https://www.marketingsociety.com/the-gym/and-so-bed%E2%80%A6#2HaSUa1ZCZr6VCgR.99

26 Lury, G (2016) [accessed 6 February 2017] And so to bed...: What we can all learn about managing customer experience from Premier Inn, *The Marketing Society* [Online] https://www.marketingsociety.com/the-gym/and-so-bed%E2%80%A6#2HaSUa1ZCZr6VCgR.99

27 Lury, G (2016) [accessed 6 February 2017] And so to bed...: What we can all learn about managing customer experience from Premier Inn, *The Marketing Society* [Online] https://www.marketingsociety.com/the-gym/and-so-bed%E2%80%A6#2HaSUa1ZCZr6VCgR.99

28 Fitzgerald, F Scott (1936) [accessed 6 February 2017] The Crack-Up, *Esquire* [Online] http://www.esquire.com/news-politics/a4310/the-crack-up/

Keeping it as simple as possible... but not any simpler

10

'The time has come,' the Walrus said,
To talk of many things:
Of shoes – and ships – and sealing-wax –,
Of cabbages – and kings –
And why the sea is boiling hot –
And whether pigs have wings.'
LEWIS CARROLL, 'THE WALRUS AND THE CARPENTER'[1]

Simple but not simplistic

'The time has come,' the author said,
To talk of many things:
Of purpose – principles – and philosophies –,
Of brands – and marketing –
And why simplicity seduces –
And whether the consumer is really king.'

This chapter will put my own advice into action, making things as simple as possible... but not any simpler.

This book set out to challenge a number of marketing 'laws', especially the idea that simplification is good but singularity even better. The Marketing Complex of the title is an ironic reference to the discipline's fixation with simplification and the dangers of the drive to oversimplification; what I have called the search for singularity.

Along the way, a number of challenges to conventional marketing thinking have been discussed.

I have put forward a new framework – the Marketing Complex Framework – as a means not only of capturing, but managing, the complexity of brands in a chaotic world. I have called for a change in the underlying mindset of marketers, suggesting they need to embrace and manage multiplicity.

So what does all that mean?

Complexity is good

'Simplification is good and complexity is bad' seems to be the mantra of the modern world. In the midst of a chaotic and complex world, people have retreated to the apparent comfort and ease of oversimplification. This is despite the fact that this can lead to bad decisions and even worse outcomes.

Unfortunately, this isn't just true of fields from music to politics to economics; the same is true in the world of marketing and branding. The search for singularity is currently revered but it is a false god.

Marketers need to embrace the complexity and learn to better manage the multiplicity of the modern world: a world where the brandscape has fundamentally altered in the last 30 years and where the rate of change is if anything accelerating. A modern brand is like an organic entity constantly growing and changing: new products and services are added; pricing and distribution change; new communications are developed and shared; new customers buy into the brand while others may be tempted away; the workforce changes. Sometimes even the brand name and/or its identity changes yet the brand remains.

A brand is therefore not a static or consistent concept but one that attains and maintains some consistency and coherency despite having porous boundaries. Brand multiplicity is a term used in this book to try to capture the true complexity and constantly evolving multifaceted nature of brands and their relationships with multiple groups of different stakeholders. Managing this brand multiplicity should be the ultimate aim for any good marketer.

Marketing isn't branding

The theory and practice of branding and marketing are fundamentally different.

Branding is conceptual and takes a longer-term perspective. It is about purpose, principles and personality and works inside out. In some ways, brands can be likened to a religion or a cult. Brands aren't generally founded on some startling new customer insight derived from market research. More often, they are the result of somebody or some people who have that 'vision thing', the vision and values to create and champion something they truly believe in.

If the development of brands is driven by the customer then there is a danger they will become homogenized: bland and not distinctive. They won't be able to play their role in providing people with choices. If marketers spend their time asking customers the same questions, in broadly the same ways, they are likely to come up with the same sorts of answers and then design the same brands. It is the differences in the beliefs and principles of the brands and the way in which they choose to behave that has, and should continue to provide their distinctiveness.

While there are an increasing number of brands that have or are defining a purpose above and beyond making returns for their shareholders, it is still far from being true for every brand. Ryanair or Primark may not be seen as serving a noble purpose beyond their core service, but it hasn't stopped them being highly successful businesses and brands.

Furthermore, even those brands that have purposes don't always have purposes that are for the betterment of the planet or the community; they are the purpose the founders believe in. Much as I applaud their purpose, BrewDog is one such example.

Marketing is more action orientated and takes a short- to mid-term perspective. It is about identifying and answering customer needs and is customer-centric. Marketing focuses on the way in which the brand goes to market, while branding is focused on defining the long-term philosophy of the brand. Therefore, when it comes to marketing the customer is 'king'. A better understanding of your customers and their motivations can help a marketer develop a better offer, a better way to engage and touch its customers, a better way to sell the brand and its purpose in a way that is appealing and motivating.

Marketing can then be seen as working out how best to translate a brand's purpose and philosophy into products and services, and how these can then be best delivered to the market in ways that will appeal to potential customers and build a relationship with them.

Branding and marketing are, however, intrinsically intertwined; marketing is the way in which the brand's purpose and philosophy is taken to market through products, services, brand communications and brand touchpoints. Marketing helps shape how the brand is perceived, what space the brand will have in the mind of the various stakeholder groups. Though in the modern world of customer-generated content and social media, marketers need to recognize that there are things they can and things they can't control directly. New brand equity and reputation management strategies need to be evolved.

The consumer isn't always king

Following naturally from the above, the customer may be king for marketing but not for branding. The mantra that you must put the customer at the heart of your brand is deceptively appealing. In taking your brand to market this is true, but when defining your brand, its philosophy and principles they are more like an important baron or prince. The brand owner is and should be king.

The abdication of ownership that appears to be going on in some businesses and for some brands is dangerous on a number of grounds:

- From a legal point of view, ownership is key to protect these valuable assets.

- From an innovation point of view, the customer can't and doesn't know what they can have or even sometimes what they want, and left in control would often kill ideas and innovations before they were formed and ready for the market.

- From a differentiation point of view – as discussed, if the role of a brand is to provide its customers, its stakeholders with choice.

If brands are put into the hands of customers it is likely that they will end up asking the same things as the other customer-'owned' brands and so commoditize the whole market. If the brands aren't distinctive then why should I choose one over the other on any grounds other than price and availability?

A framework not another model

Too many of the current brand models are no longer fit for purpose. They are closer to brand proposition models and simply aren't very good for brand definition and positioning.

What I have argued is that a new model, or rather, a new framework – the Marketing Complex Framework – is required. I've used the word framework not only because it differentiates from what has gone before but because it suggests a larger concept. A framework is the description of an underlying structure of a whole system while a

Figure 10.1 The new Marketing Complex Framework

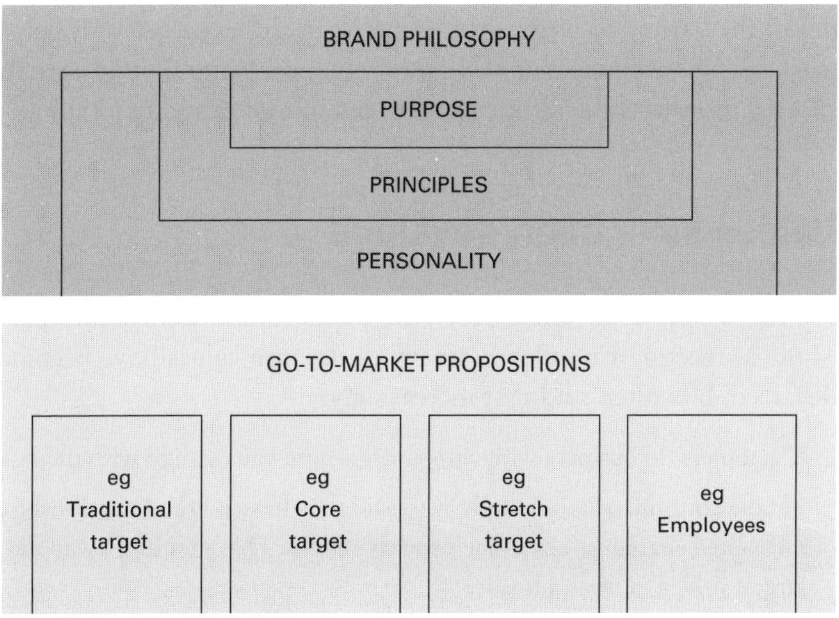

SOURCE The Value Engineers (2017)

model tends to be a more simplified representation or version of an idea (Figure 10.1).

The framework allows for not only a separation between the more long-term and consistent core of a brand, the brand's philosophy, but for a number of shorter-term more changeable specific propositions that all sit under that one brand name. It aligns with the notion of brand multiplicity and the idea that a brand is like an organic entity that is not a static or consistent concept but one that attains some consistency and coherency despite constantly changing and having porous boundaries.

The two sections of the framework are the brand positioning made up of the brand's purpose, principles and positioning and a series of go-to-market propositions, with the key difference being that there are more than one of these and that they don't have to be (though they can be) single-minded in themselves.

A go-to-market proposition is similar to the core of many current brand models, but a difference is that a framework facilitates and encourages marketers to think about multiple propositions simultaneously coexisting so providing more depth and variety to the total brand narrative.

This separation of the two elements is crucial, as it is this flexibility that allows this new multipart framework to handle the complexities of the variety of target groups and their different needs. It helps marketers manage the complexity that a modern brand must have to succeed. It reflects the difference between branding and marketing.

Values have been devalued

Principles not values are a key part of the brand philosophy part of the Marketing Complex Framework because values have become devalued. It is often said that increasingly:

'Customers do business with companies whose values align with theirs.'[2]

'Of the consumers in our study who said they have a brand relationship, 64% cited shared values as the primary reason. That's far and away the largest driver (of brand loyalty).'[3]

Whether or not these statistics actually show this is happening in practice and not just in claimed behaviour is debatable but there does appear to be some movement in this direction.

The real problem is that every marketer seems to believe this and so is defining their values in ways that they know will appeal to their customers, which the organizations behind their brands will sign up for and which are acceptable to their investors. This has led to a situation where too many brands are claiming the same 'motherhood and apple pie' values like integrity, respect, caring for people and innovative.

So something needs to change and the alternative suggestion is to focus on a brand's beliefs or principles. It's too easy for a brand to say that it has what are often loosely defined generic values that are difficult to measure. If you express your beliefs, you have something to live up to and be measured by. A belief or principle drives action and, as the old saying goes, actions speak louder than words. If a brand has principles, it has things to which it is truly committed and is willing to stick to, even if it means it is more expensive to do or it closes down an opportunity.

A principle isn't really a principle until it costs you money. It may cost you something in the short term, but its real advantage is that customers take much more notice of principles in action than claimed values. Clear principles that translate into real manifestations help define and differentiate one brand from another and then, indeed, they are likely to drive choice and loyalty.

Marketers need to kick their addiction

The search for oversimplification has become an addiction for many marketers. It's an addiction that affects many aspects of their job, from brand positioning to proposition development, from insights to innovation.

It's a habit that these marketers now need to kick. Brands are complex, marketing is complicated, and people are, well, people and we know how contrary they can be.

So I encourage you to work with the notion of multiplicity for the next 66 days and see if you can establish new habits.

Having said that, many of the traditional attributes of a good marketer, including the 5Cs – Collaboration, Customer-centricity, Commercial acumen, Cleverness and good Communications – will still be required, but there is an urgent need for marketers to more readily accept ambiguity and set out to actively manage multiplicity. They need to challenge the so-called immutable laws of branding and marketing, and realize that many of the previously and often blindly accepted truths no longer hold true or at least don't hold true all the time.

A brand doesn't need a single-minded proposition, it needs a range of compelling propositions tailored to different stakeholder groups. The customer isn't always king.

There is still a need for customer-centricity in marketing and benefits to be had from simplification, but if you think this contradicts the arguments set out in the book then either you haven't understood what I have been saying or you have been oversimplifying my arguments.

Notes

1 Carroll, L (1872) *Through the Looking-Glass and What Alice Found There*, 1st edn, Macmillan, London

2 Claveria, K (2014) [accessed 14 March 2017] What motivates customers to choose one brand over another? *Vision Critical* [Online] https://www.visioncritical.com/bruce-philp-webinar-recap/

3 Ciotti, G (2014) [accessed 14 March 2017] The Shocking Truth: Customers don't want to engage with your company, *Entrepreneur* [Online] https://www.entrepreneur.com/article/234326

What's next? 11

'*It is better to debate a question without settling it than to settle a question without debating it.*'
JOSEPH JOUBERT IN *THE NOTEBOOKS OF JOSEPH JOUBERT*[1]

Not the beginning of the end but maybe the end of the beginning

My brother Adam, co-founder of HHCL + Partners, wrote in *Marketing at a Point of Change* that:

'The point of purchase isn't the end of the sale, it is the beginning of a relationship.'[2]

Taking that thought and adapting it, I would like to suggest that:

Reading this book is unlikely to be the end of the debate; I hope it is the beginning of a discussion.

I recognize that there are many very talented marketers out there doing a difficult job, brilliantly. There are some who are already managing multiplicity. For them, this book may seem like closing the stable door after the horse has bolted.

Unfortunately, while they are off and running, there are still lots of other 'horses' still milling around in their boxes, in the stable. There are marketers who still persist in doing things in the same old ways, using the same old models. I believe they are holding back their brands by clinging on to out-of-date ways of thinking.

I want to challenge them to challenge themselves. To challenge the old ways and find new and better ways to deal with the reality of the chaotic world we live in and the complexity of modern marketing.

I would welcome challenges and debate. I have set out arguments for which I don't have absolute proof, because the methods and ideas I've put forward are still evolving. I'm not trying to invent new marketing 'laws', I don't believe in such things, but the aim of the book and its arguments is to provide guidance on better practice for brand development and management.

I have made the case for managing brand multiplicity. I doubt everyone will be immediately convinced by everything I have suggested, but I hope they will consider it and enter into the debate.

Ultimately, my hope is for marketing to take its place (or have more of a place) in the C-Suite: for marketing and branding to demonstrate how they can separately and together add value to organizations by simplifying things as much as possible... but not any more.

I believe that branding, as defined here, needs to be at the heart of every organization and that good marketing is required to make those brands successful and sustainable. To do so marketers need to overcome their current simplicity complex.

The best companies will not just be high-performance organizations (HPOs) but high-performance brands (HPBs), and one of the pillars for an HPB will be the ability to manage multiplicity.

Notes

1 Joubert, J (2006) *The Notebooks of Joseph Joubert*, 1st edn, New York Review Books Classics, New York

2 Lury, A (1996) *Marketing at a Point of Change*, 1st edn, Howell Henry Chaldecott Lury and Partners, London

INDEX

Note: The index is filed in alphabetical, word-by-word order. Within main headings, numbers and the prefix 'Mc' are filed as spelt out in full. Acronyms and 'Mr' are filed as written. Page locators in *italics* denote information contained within a Figure or Table.